I KNOW WHY SHE STAYED

Reader's Guide

FIRST EDITION

Copyright © 2024 – Everyone Needs Roger, Kasey Rogers, K. J. Harrowick and Justine Manzano

No part of this book may be reproduced, distributed, or transmitted in any form or by any means, including photocopying, recording, or other electronic or mechanical methods, without the prior written permission of the authors, except as permitted by U.S. copyright law and the Fair Use Act for classroom education. For permission requests or classroom speaking engagements, contact the authors at: contactus@iknowwhyshestayed.org.

Library of Congress Control Number: 2025904344

ISBN: 979-8991624756

"Sometimes it is easier to see the trauma in others than it is in our own lives. It is in reading that we find validation. And in I Know Why She Stayed I had that experience, over and over. I did not know the term "economic abuse" but I have suffered from it. It is that shared experience that gives us words and power, for if we can name it, we can mourn what we lost, allow ourselves to feel rage, and finally release our pain and say, 'never again.'"

- Lara Lillibridge, author of *The Truth About Unringing Phones: Essays on Yearning* and *Girlish: Growing Up in a Lesbian Home*

INTRODUCTION

Welcome to the Reader's Guide for the memoir, *I Know Why She Stayed*. Throughout the Reader's Guide we will take you into the lives of Kasey Rogers and K. J. Harrowick, two authors who experienced financial and domestic abuse firsthand. With a series of case files, we'll unpack and examine small moments in their lives to better understand what these two women endured and how it affects them.

Let's imagine for a moment that you've just purchased a puzzle. On the box is the image of a smiling woman. She is surrounded by family, a home, and maybe even a pet or two, but when you look in her eyes, there is no smile.

Ask yourself, why isn't she smiling? Perhaps this puzzle holds a secret.

As you scatter the pieces across the table, you find your first clue. The image printed on the pieces does not match the woman shown on the box. What's even stranger is that this puzzle doesn't seem to follow the same rules as others you've pieced together before. Each piece is the same shape, and while you search for the edges, it's only to find that none exist.

Author Bob Corrigan says, "The reason it's unlike any puzzle you're familiar with is because each piece of this puzzle is in fact one of the woman's memories, a discrete event she has personally endured. Her memories—each one a piece of the puzzle—extend from the moment she was born until the day the photo on the front of the box was taken. As you connect each piece with another, the truth of her life—the real truth—starts to take shape, and you begin to understand the abuse she has endured. You see her not as she appears on the cover of the puzzle box, but as she truly is."

A victim. A survivor. A warrior. This helps you understand *why* she hides behind her smile.

According to Dr. Edie Zusman, MD, a trauma-trained neurosurgeon at the Piedmont Neuroscience Center and Domestics Shelters, "a repeated cycle of abuse by a partner [or parent], whether physical or non-physical, results in trauma and affects the brain to such a degree that memories of that abuse become fragmented, like blurry photos or books with pages missing. Survivors are certain something bad has happened, but when asked for exact specifics and timelines, their memories seem to have lost those details."[1]

When we connect the dots, this is what makes the comparison between the mind of a domestic abuse victim and a puzzle so helpful: each piece is a fragment of the whole and only makes sense when all the pieces are considered together. One piece—or even a handful—can't reveal the whole picture or tell the whole story. But if those few pieces are all you're shown, that's all you see, like the smile a victim hides behind.

In this Reader's Guide, we will explore two puzzles as case files for Kasey Rogers and K. J. Harrowick, who both suffered financial and domestic abuse as revealed in their memoir *I Know Why She Stayed*. This guide will help us study the cycle of abuse as well as the big and small instances which showcase the stark reality of how these events shaped their personalities, their traumas, and their lives.

To help readers navigate the case files, we've included a glossary which provides a more in-depth explanation of the terms used. It connects each type of abusive tactic with a case file that examines a specific passage within the memoir, *I Know Why She Stayed*.

We use direct language instead of softening the term for an individual who commits acts to harm another person—**abusers**—regardless of whether those acts are physical, mental, sexual, financial, or any combination of these together. Studies of abuser tactics have shown how they maintain power and control over others, with an end goal to control, disrespect, and undermine their victim's confidence and independence. To refer to them as anything other than what they are—abusers—is a disservice to the people they harm, and continue to damage, sabotage, misuse, and malign.

Under the Microscope:
[1] A. Kippert, "Fragmented memories: How trauma can cause memory loss." domesticshelters.org, July 1, 2024,
https://www.domesticshelters.org/articles/health/fragmented-memories-how-trauma-can-cause-memory-loss

THE CYCLE OF ABUSE

The best way to solve a puzzle is to begin with a pattern, which helps to organize and define shared characteristics.

Domestic abuse also comes in patterns. The first helps to lock victims into the Invisible Trap, and the second keeps them in it. We'll begin by discussing how this Invisible Trap works and why the patterns are so effective. In this section you'll learn about the role of empathy in violent relationships, establishing trust and how it leads to destabilization and mistrust, positions of power and the effects of self-doubt, and how these abuser tactics lure even the smartest, most savvy women into the invisible traps that keep them caged.

Cycle 1: The Lockup

Abusers love to be in control. It gives them power, confidence, and helps keep their lives ordered the way *they* like it, with little to no empathy for others, according to the research study "The Role of Empathy in Violent Intimate Relationships" conducted by Emilio C. Ulloa and Julia F. Hammett. The study's conclusion "suggests that a lack of empathy, including a lack of sympathy, sensitivity, understanding, and compassion, may translate into adverse behaviors, such as overall intimate partner violence."[2]

Abusers begin with a Lure, which can take the shape of kindness, romance, and often a charismatic, trustworthy persona. They put on the face of a good citizen, or a false identity, and in many cases hold a position of power, as seen in K. J. Harrowick's case files where she was still a child living under her father's authority.

Once trust is established between abuser and victim, the next step is Destabilization. This is where emotional abuse draws power with tactics such as blending positive and negative comments, shaming and blaming, manipulation, and twisting lies and truth until the victim begins to doubt their sanity and innocence. Once those roots take hold, victims fall prey to the same tactic echoing in their own thoughts, thus dragging them one step deeper into The Lockup.

When a victim's self-esteem disappears, it grants the abuser shielding to get away with continued abuse and violence.

The next step is Isolation, or cutting off victims from their friends, family, support, medical aid, and finances. This leads to the victim's dependence on their abuser for love, support, and basic needs. This can also extend to isolating victims from childcare, jobs, or education, thus reinforcing dependency.

The last step in The Lockup pattern is Violence, which takes on many forms: sexual, physical, and in some cases, murder. With each step in The Lockup pattern, a victim's life is in greater danger, and once they're locked in, a new pattern emerges.

Cycle 2: The Invisible Trap

According to Safe Family Justice Centers, The Invisible Trap is "a repeating pattern that keeps victims trapped in harmful relationships. This cycle often involves periods of tension-building, explosive incidents, reconciliation, and calm."[3]

This cyclical cycle of events reinforces self-doubt, isolation, and dependency in victims, as seen in the case files of Kasey Rogers. After moments of reprieve and calm, and often loving and charismatic behavior from her husband, the tension would begin to build, and the cycle begin anew.

Under the Microscope:
2 Emilio C. Ulloa and Julia F. Hammett, "The Role of Empathy in Violent Intimate Relationships," National Library of Medicine, January 7, 2016, https://pmc.ncbi.nlm.nih.gov/articles/PMC10500614/

3 safe_admin, "Understanding the Cycle of Abuse: Recognizing Patterns and Seeking Help," Safe Family Justice Centers of Riverside, June 26, 2024, https://www.safefjc.org/understanding-the-cycle-of-abuse-recognizing-patterns-and-seeking-help/

THE PUZZLE PIECES OF
I KNOW WHY SHE STAYED

To fully understand the life experiences of each woman—our victims—the puzzle pieces must be assembled. To facilitate your study, each "piece" is color-coded and attached to "case files." The exploration of each case file will include passages that display evidence of abuse and its effects, that displays evidence taken directly from the memoir, *I Know Why She Stayed*, multiple behaviors and tactics used by abusers, and reference text to help us understand how each memory, or puzzle piece, is linked to domestic and financial abuse, and its effects on the victim long after the events take place.

PSYCHOLOGICAL & EMOTIONAL ABUSE

CASE FILE 1: Coercive Control
CASE FILE 2: Manipulation
CASE FILE 3: False Identity
CASE FILE 4: Financial Abuse
CASE FILE 5: Façade of Equality
CASE FILE 6: Social Stigma
CASE FILE 7: Victimhood
CASE FILE 8: Destruction of Self-Esteem
CASE FILE 9: Conditional Love
CASE FILE 10: Double Standard
CASE FILE 11: The Façade of the "Nice Guy"
CASE FILE 12: Minimization and Rationalization
CASE FILE 13: Abandonment
CASE FILE 14: Devalued
CASE FILE 15: Gaslighting
CASE FILE 16: Isolation
CASE FILE 17: Intimidation
CASE FILE 18: Lying
CASE FILE 19: Guilt
CASE FILE 20: Controlling Assets
CASE FILE 22: Blame Shifting
CASE FILE 23: Threats
CASE FILE 24: Financial Infidelity
CASE FILE 25: Racking Up Debt
CASE FILE 26: Financial Trauma
CASE FILE 27: Post-Traumatic Stress Disorder
CASE FILE 28: Humiliation
CASE FILE 29: Gaslighting
CASE FILE 30: Financial Sabotage
CASE FILE 31: Emotional Abuse
CASE FILE 32: Victim Blaming
CASE FILE 33: Obstacles
CASE FILE 34: Minimizing
CASE FILE 35: The Good Guy Behavior
CASE FILE 36: Dominance Hierarchies
CASE FILE 38: Transactional Manipulation
CASE FILE 40: Minimizing Feelings
CASE FILE 41: Subjugation
CASE FILE 43: Technology-Assisted Domestic Abuse
CASE FILE 44: Insults
CASE FILE 45: Power Imbalance
CASE FILE 46: Post-Traumatic Stress Disorder
CASE FILE 47: Chronic Stress
CASE FILE 48: Weaponization of Guilt
CASE FILE 49: Conditional Love
CASE FILE 50: Narcissism
CASE FILE 51: Name Calling
CASE FILE 52: Double Standard
CASE FILE 53: Spiritual Abuse
CASE FILE 54: Weaponization of Family, Children and Pets

FINANCIAL & ECONOMIC ABUSE

CASE FILE 4: Financial abuse
CASE FILE 10: Double Standard
CASE FILE 13: Abandonment
CASE FILE 15: Gaslighting
CASE FILE 20: Controlling Assets
CASE FILE 21: Controlling Employment
CASE FILE 22: Blame Shifting
CASE FILE 23: Threats
CASE FILE 24: Financial Infidelity
CASE FILE 25: Racking Up Debt
CASE FILE 26: Financial Trauma
CASE FILE 28: Humiliation
CASE FILE 30: Financial Sabotage
CASE FILE 31: Emotional Abuse
CASE FILE 35: The Good Guy Behavior
CASE FILE 37: Withholding Money
CASE FILE 39: Financial Gatekeeping
CASE FILE 43: Technology-Assisted Domestic Abuse
CASE FILE 46: Post-Traumatic Stress Disorder
CASE FILE 50: Narcissism
CASE FILE 54: Weaponization of Family, Children and Pets

Additional Ways Abusers Use Financial Abuse to Entrap Victims

- Berate victim for small spending
- Forbid victim from working
- Force victim to obtain loans
- Hide Assets
- Rack up or hide debit
- Refuse to pay child support
- Refuse to pay for basic necessities
- Ruin credit history
- Steal victim's assets
- Unpaid labor in family business

FALSE IDENTITIES

There are two types of **false identities** presented. One is created by the abuser who degrades, humiliates, dehumanizes, and isolates their victim. When this happens on a consistent basis, the victim begins to believe their abuser's lies and see themselves as the abuser does. The abuser might paint the same image of their victim for others making it more difficult for them to speak out because they fear they won't be believed. The victim begins to have a false self-image, and they begin to think, act, and respond in ways that erase their true identity as they only see themselves in the context of the abuser's image of them.

Abusers work hard to control the narrative about themselves so they can maintain their charming, charismatic, "good guy" image. They might appear to be a devoted partner, a loving family man or be revered by friends, family and colleagues. But behind this "good guy" façade is the real person that uses this image to hide behind the truth. The persona of the "good guy" leaves others disbelieving the victims when they speak out. It leaves the victim feeling confused, isolated, and is a major reason they stay trapped in the cycle of abuse.

CASE FILE 1: Coercive Control
CASE FILE 2: Manipulation
CASE FILE 3: False Identity
CASE FILE 5: Façade of Equality
CASE FILE 7: Victimhood
CASE FILE 10: Double Standard
CASE FILE 11: The Façade of the "Nice Guy"
CASE FILE 18: Lying
CASE FILE 22: Blame Shifting
CASE FILE 31: Emotional Abuse
CASE FILE 32: Victim Blaming
CASE FILE 34: Minimizing

CASE FILE 35: The Good Guy Behavior
CASE FILE 36: Dominance Hierarchies
CASE FILE 42: The Two Faces of Narcissists
CASE FILE 43: Technology- Assisted Domestic Abuse
CASE FILE 48: Weaponization of Guilt
CASE FILE 50: Narcissism
CASE FILE 51: Name Calling
CASE FILE 52: Double Standard
CASE FILE 53: Spiritual Abuse
CASE FILE 54: Weaponization of Family, Children and Pets

OBSTACLES

That prevent a victim from escape

Throughout the memoir *I Know Why She Stayed*, authors Kasey Rogers and K. J. Harrowick face obstacles that prevent them from moving forward in life in a positive way because of the financial trauma they experienced.

Abusive tactics, outside influences, and reinforced self-images create obstacles which prevent them from escape. They become caught in a labyrinth, isolated and alone.

CASE FILE 6: Social Stigma
CASE FILE 20: Controlling Assets
CASE FILE 21: Controlling Employment
CASE FILE 23: Threats
CASE FILE 25: Racking Up Debt
CASE FILE 28: Humiliation
CASE FILE 33: Obstacles
CASE FILE 35: The Good Guy Behavior
CASE FILE 36: Dominance Hierarchies
CASE FILE 37: Withholding Money
CASE FILE 41: Subjugation
CASE FILE 43: Technology-Assisted Domestic Abuse

CASE FILE 44: Insults
CASE FILE 47: Chronic Stress
CASE FILE 48: Weaponization of Guilt
CASE FILE 49: Conditional Love
CASE FILE 50: Narcissism
CASE FILE 51: Name Calling
CASE FILE 52: Double Standard
CASE FILE 53: Spiritual Abuse
CASE FILE 54: Weaponization of Family, Children and Pets

CONTROL

One of the main reasons it is difficult for victims to leave an abusive relationship is the impact of Coercive Control. The behavior is defined as an act or a pattern of assault, threats, humiliation and intimidation or other abuse that is used to harm, punish, or frighten their victim.

Coercive and controlling behavior is at the heart of domestic abuse because it traumatizes the victim so their actions may not reflect an accurate articulation of their experiences.

CASE FILE 1: Coercive Control
CASE FILE 2: Manipulation
CASE FILE 4: Financial abuse
CASE FILE 8: Destruction of Self-Esteem
CASE FILE 12: Minimization and Rationalization
CASE FILE 14: Devalued
CASE FILE 16: Isolation
CASE FILE 17: Intimidation
CASE FILE 18: Lying
CASE FILE 19: Guilt
CASE FILE 20: Controlling Assets
CASE FILE 21: Controlling Employment

CASE FILE 23: Threats
CASE FILE 26: Financial Trauma
CASE FILE 27: Post-Traumatic Stress Disorder
CASE FILE 30: Financial Sabotage
CASE FILE 31: Emotional Abuse
CASE FILE 32: Victim Blaming
CASE FILE 33: Obstacles
CASE FILE 37: Withholding Money
CASE FILE 39: Financial Gatekeeping
CASE FILE 47: Chronic Stress
CASE FILE 50: Narcissism
CASE FILE 52: Double Standard

REFLECTIONS

Throughout the memoir, *I Know Why She Stayed*, authors Kasey Rogers and K. J. Harrowick begin to realize the various ways their abusers maintain control or strategies to defend their actions. These realizations lead to moments of deep reflection, in which both authors struggled to understand the reality of what they'd been through and how they ended up in an abusive relationship.

CASE FILE 3: False Identity
CASE FILE 9: Conditional Love
CASE FILE 15: Gaslighting
CASE FILE 16: Isolation
CASE FILE 18: Lying
CASE FILE 24: Financial Infidelity
CASE FILE 26: Financial Trauma
CASE FILE 31: Emotional Abuse
CASE FILE 32: Victim Blaming

CASE FILE 35: The Good Guy Behavior
CASE FILE 36: Dominance Hierarchies
CASE FILE 38: Transactional Manipulation
CASE FILE 41: Subjugation
CASE FILE 45: Power Imbalance
CASE FILE 47: Chronic Stress
CASE FILE 48: Weaponization of Guilt
CASE FILE 49: Conditional Love

SURVIVAL STRATEGIES

Just because victims know something is very wrong with their relationship doesn't mean they can leave. When they become stuck, victims of abuse often need to find strategies to survive with an abusive partner or parent until they can make their escape. These Survival Strategies and coping mechanisms help them find limited bursts of peace or safety, even if it means acting outside of their normal character.

CASE FILE 1: Coercive Control
CASE FILE 2: Manipulation
CASE FILE 13: Abandonment
CASE FILE 20: Controlling Assets
CASE FILE 21: Controlling Employment
CASE FILE 22: Blame Shifting
CASE FILE 23: Threats
CASE FILE 24: Financial Infidelity
CASE FILE 26: Financial Trauma
CASE FILE 27: Post-Traumatic Stress Disorder
CASE FILE 31: Emotional Abuse
CASE FILE 33: Obstacles
CASE FILE 47: Chronic Stress

SELF-ADVOCACY

As authors Kasey Rogers and K. J. Harrowick reflected on their experiences and pushed through using survival strategies, they each fought for their freedom from the terrible circumstances they were trapped in. These moments of self-advocacy sometimes failed, and sometimes succeeded. But they are a key part of finding escape from the cage of abuse.

CASE FILE 2: Manipulation
CASE FILE 12: Minimization and Rationalization
CASE FILE 15: Gaslighting
CASE FILE 18: Lying
CASE FILE 21: Controlling Employment
CASE FILE 22: Blame Shifting
CASE FILE 23: Threats

CASE FILE 30: Financial Sabotage
CASE FILE 31: Emotional Abuse
CASE FILE 43: Technology-Assisted Domestic Abuse
CASE FILE 44: Insults
CASE FILE 50: Narcissism

The Case Files

CASE FILE 1
Evidence: Coercive Control

The ultimate goal of abusive behavior is power and control over the actions of another individual. Abusers often display their belief that they should be able to control all elements of the victim's time.[4]

I heard Phillip's familiar voice, heavy with recrimination.

"Well, I guess you've already left to go to Jenny's. Funny how you always have time to spend with your friends. Don't bother calling me back tonight. I'm sure you'll be staying out late. Well, I have to get up early tomorrow because I work for a living. Call me tomorrow when you finish packing, so we…"

I erased the rest of the message without listening to the end. It would only be another reminder of the countless times during our marriage when Phillip insisted my desire to attend any social function was selfish and that doing so made me a terrible wife and mother.

Under the Microscope:
4 P. Lehmann, C. A. Simmons, & V. K. Pillai, "The Validation of the Checklist of Controlling Behaviors (CCB): Assessing Coercive Control in Abusive Relationships," Sage Journals, September 23, 2012, https://doi.org/10.1177/1077801212456522

CASE FILE 2
Evidence: Manipulation

Manipulation is coercive or unethical behavior driven by the goal of exploiting or controlling another person for their own personal gain.[5,6]

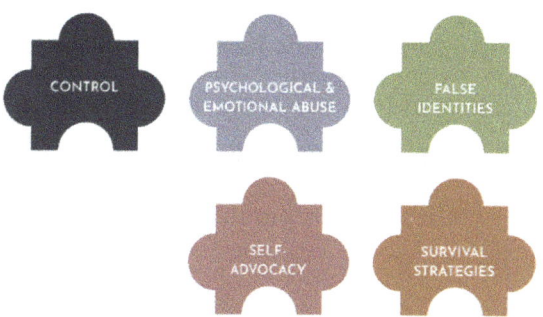

It wasn't long before I logged into his email account and read them [Phillip's emails] without an iota of guilt.

What Phillip had written to various friends and family members left me numb. His tone invoked sheer hostility whenever his correspondence mentioned me. He made claims about my actions or inactions that revealed a resentment built on complete fabrications. Of particular note was an email he sent to his sister, Rachel. Phillip claimed I had squandered all the money from the sale of our house in the States on a "failed" business and that I had refused to follow through in contacting an attorney about our residency status in Canada.

I wanted to scream when I read that. How dare he! None of his claims were true.

Under the Microscope:
5 K. Vogel, "How to Spot Manipulation Tactics," Psych Central, September 9, 2024, https://psychcentral.com/health/tactics-manipulators-use-to-win-and-confuse-you

6 Harriet Braiker, *Who's Pulling Your Strings?: How to Break the Cycle of Manipulation and Regain Control of Your Life*, (McGraw-Hill, 2005)

CASE FILE 3
Evidence: False Self-Identity

Abusers present negative impressions of the victim to undermine their self-esteem and to create false impressions that bolster their ability to manipulate the narrative.[7]

Standing in the tiny kitchen, my anger boiled over. I feared I would revert to the person I was when I had first arrived in Alexandria once I moved back to the U.S. The self-doubt and loathing faded only when Phillip wasn't there to present his image of me. I realized I had absorbed all the negative messages Phillip had sent me during our marriage when he attacked my character. In his absence, I had regained my confidence.

While I sipped my drink, I imagined dozens of dubious reasons Phillip wanted us to return to the States since this arrangement had suited him just fine for years. Yet, there was a part of me that wanted to go back in time. I yearned to retreat to the days before I had realized that none of the reasons Phillip initially gave me for his living six hours away made sense. I longed to erase the knowledge that he most likely had been lying to me for years. Now that I suspected why he wanted to be so far away, I couldn't shut out the thoughts that forced me to wonder why I hadn't seen it all along.

Under the Microscope:
7 S. Flannery, "When an Abuser Controls the Story," domesticshelters.org, July 1, 2024, (2024, July 1). https://www.domesticshelters.org/articles/identifying-abuse/when-an-abuser-controls-the-story

CASE FILE 4
Evidence: Financial Abuse

Economic abuse includes exerting control over income, spending, bank accounts, bills, employment, housing and borrowing.[8]

In March of 2010, he'd [Phillip] taken a new job as a creative director for an ad firm in Albany, New York. I assumed he would happily continue our awkward arrangement of living separately. That wasn't the case. His attitude shifted dramatically, and he began overtly referring to the move north as a mistake and suggesting that it had been my idea.

He [Phillip] complained bitterly about missing the twins' childhood and insinuated that because the café wasn't making enough income to live on, it forced him to get a job back in the States to support our family. Then, he did something that thoroughly alarmed me. He opened a separate bank account that I had no access to. He claimed I'd overdrafted our joint statement. At first, I tried to reason with him. After all, he was the one who'd made the unrecorded transaction that hadn't been posted to the account. That led to my assuming we had more funds available than we did. Regardless, he blamed me, and shortly after that, he closed our joint account because he said he needed to "put his foot down because I was financially irresponsible."

In April, he told me he would no longer contribute to paying any of the bills in Canada. He said it was a waste of "his money." The mortgage, taxes, and other building overhead, including all expenses related to his children, were now my sole responsibility. This made me furious, but it opened my eyes. Now I knew he was hiding something—I just didn't know what.

Then Phillip demanded the Beans and I move to the Albany area.

Under the Microscope:
8 Shannon Thomas LCSW, *Exposing Financial Abuse: When Money is a Weapon* (MAST Publishing House, June 26, 2018)

CASE FILE 5
Evidence: Façade of Equality

An abuser will often start off the relationship by presenting themselves as caring, kind and helpful. This makes them appear to be a wonderful partner and creates a sense of trust with the victim. Abusers use flattery and love bombing to convince their victim they are special.[9]

What I appreciated most about Phillip initially was how different he acted from many of the men I'd worked with in the past. I always seemed to work alongside this fraternal pack of grown boys who barely recognized their female colleagues as co-workers. Many of the women I worked with got smaller projects and lower salaries.

Phillip, however, treated me more seriously, both personally and professionally.

One of the reasons I started my own business was I got sick to death of being just as skilled as my male counterparts without getting the credit for my work. It seemed like I only got positive feedback when I wore something that showed off my figure. I heard the whispers and tried to laugh off the uncomfortable banter my male co-workers called jokes.

Under the Microscope:
9 NLS Admin, "How Abusers Use Manipulation in Relationships to Control Their Partner," National Legal Service Solicitors, March 16, 2023, https://nationallegalservice.co.uk/how- abusers-use-manipulation-in-relationships-to-control-their- partner/

CASE FILE 6
Evidence: Social Stigma

Social stigmas can create artificial barriers to confronting relationship conflicts. They often conflate issues to allow abusers to manipulate circumstances to deflect responsibility.[10]

In this passage, Kasey has just broken the news to Phillip that she's pregnant. Gauging Phillip's reaction to this news shows how he uses guilt and his own religious ideologies to control the narrative.

[Phillip speaking]: "Well, it's not the news I expected. What happens here is your decision, but I am hoping you'll decide not to have an abortion. It's the whole Catholic thing. Other than that, Kasey, I don't know what to say about the situation."

I moved the food around on my plate. I didn't press him, knowing the news was a shock. I'd had weeks to process everything. He'd only had a few minutes, so I let him be. He left shortly after that without saying much. I cried endlessly over the next few days when I didn't hear from him. When he finally called, he didn't even bring up the subject.

I was riddled with guilt, believing I had ruined Phillip's life. It didn't occur to me then that we were both responsible for the situation and this life-altering news affected me, too. Regardless, humiliation overtook me. The religious upbringing of my childhood made me believe that unplanned pregnancy made me a bad person, and I was ashamed that, despite taking birth control, I still got pregnant. I fell into a state of constant anxiety, struggling to decide what to do.

Under the Microscope:
Michael R Kramer, Carol J Rowland Hogue, and Laura M D Gaydos, "Noncontracepting behavior in women at risk for unintended pregnancy: what's religion got to do with it?," National Library of Medicine, March 28, 2007, https://pubmed.ncbi.nlm.nih.gov/17395484/

CASE FILE 7
Evidence: Victimhood

Abusers often portray themselves as innocent victims of another individuals' hurtful assessment of their character. They abdicate any responsibility for their poor behavior in relationships by suggesting they are the true victims of another person's lack of judgment of their true character.[11]

In this passage, Philip expresses a need to preserve his and Kasey's marriage with his parents by withholding the truth from them. He believes he was the victim of unfair treatment in many situations. This tactic became a pattern in marriage. Through the passages below, consider exploring why Phillip kept his marriage to Kasey a secret.

In January of 1986, we said our vows before a justice of the peace. I was several months pregnant at that point, and it seemed like he wanted to raise a child. He moved into my attic apartment, and we started our life together.

The cracks in the relationship started soon after that. The biggest one was that Phillip refused to tell anyone other than his sister Rachel that we were married. While he told his close friends and colleagues at work, he kept the rest of his family in the dark. Phillip wouldn't even tell them we were living together. Instead, he told layer upon layer of lies to conceal his secrets.

The awkwardness of this was detrimental. I'd told my friends and family members that we'd gotten married. I didn't tell them why but knew they'd figure that out soon enough. It was hard to keep track of who knew we were married and who didn't.

"Are you planning on telling your folks we got married?"

"You don't know my mother very well," he told me. "This news will ruin the weekend. I'm already the black sheep of the family. I'd rather not contribute to my already shocking reputation," he told me.

I reasoned that he knew them better than I did, but it bothered me.

Under the Microscope:
11 Dr. George K. Simon Ph.D., *In Sheep's Clothing: Understanding and Dealing with Manipulative People* (Parkhurst Brothers Publishers Inc, April 1, 2010

CASE FILE 8
Evidence: Destruction of Self-Esteem

Abusers often take aim at their victim's self-esteem because these tactics destroy one's self-confidence, making their victims easier to control. Victims internalize the negative messages sent by their abusers and begin to believe the false narrative of their abuser.[12]

Phillip undermines Kasey's confidence in their relationship and sets a trap to isolate her because the secret and subsequent lies reinforce the need to keep their two families apart.

[Phillip] continued to avoid telling his parents we got married. I couldn't understand why telling his parents the truth had been so daunting.

I started to believe he was somehow ashamed of me, which wreaked havoc on my self-confidence. I believed that, at any time, he could decide to end the marriage if I gave him a reason. At some point, and without much fanfare, I somehow went from being his girlfriend to being his fiancé. When we visited Marblehead, where his parents lived, I removed my wedding ring and put on my engagement ring.

Phillip's concealment of our marital status from his family also meant keeping our two families apart. My family and friends became secondary in all matters related to things we did as a couple. It had set up a dynamic in our relationship where I was erased. My traditions and experiences weren't a part of us. I assimilated into his world to accommodate his lie. He said, "I love you," but what did that mean if he couldn't even tell his parents that we got married and why?

Under the Microscope:
12 Lundy Bancroft, *Why Does He Do That?: Inside the Minds of Angry and Controlling Men* (Berkley Books; Reprint edition, September 2, 2003)

CASE FILE 9
Evidence: Conditional Love

Abusers use the tactic of conditional love to control the actions and reactions of their victim by promoting the notion that the victim is only worthy of their love if they behave in certain ways. Otherwise, love is withheld and fear is created that they'll risk losing the abuser's affection.[13]

Here we see the erasing of self as Kasey tries to balance the love she has for Phillip and the reality of the damage done by his conditional love.

I didn't mind our awkward arrangement most of the time, because I loved him. Phillip made me laugh, and we had great fun together exploring New York City and dreaming of the days ahead when we were both established in our creative careers. But in many ways, I didn't feel like we were married.

Looking back, I realized that my inability to confront him about money established an imbalance in our relationship. I believed he felt trapped back then and stayed with me because he needed my help to further his career. In the early days of our marriage, it made me try harder to please him. I thought if I proved I was worthy of his love, he'd love me the way I loved him.

Under the Microscope:
13 C. Wozny, "Conditional Love Is Verbally Abusive," HealthyPlace, February 1, 2024, https://www.healthyplace.com/blogs/verbalabuseinrelationships/2024/2/conditional-love-is-verbally-abusive

CASE FILE 10
Evidence: Double Standard

Double standards are used by abusers to assert what they believe are their rights but disregard them as rights that apply to other individuals.[14]

Kasey is speaking with her friends at the farewell dinner and reveals she found the passwords to his email accounts.

"I couldn't believe it. I wish he'd jotted down his bank account information. I don't even know how much he's making in this new job. Of course, he's hounding me about getting the packing done. He completely ignores that I had the kids and a business to contend with up until a week ago. He's sitting in an air-conditioned office, writing advertising copy. He thinks it's nothing to pack in this heat."

"Has he offered to come up and help you?" Carole asked.

"Nope. He said he would come up last weekend but then called me and told me he had to work."

Under the Microscope:
14 Evan Stark, *Coercive Control: How Men Entrap Women in Personal Life (Interpersonal Violence)*, (Oxford University Press; 1st edition, March 1, 2009)

CASE FILE 11
Evidence: The Façade of the "Nice Guy"

Inside the façade of a nice guy hides the same insidious selfish abuser who exhibits coercive control over their victims by appearing to be someone they're not. Their partners know their behaviors show the same sense of entitlement as regular narcissism.[15]

At the farewell party, Kasey tells her friends Phillip opened up a separate bank account.

Even though Carole has no real relationship with Phillip, she assumes he is a nice guy having met him a few times. Abusers know how to manipulate self-image, which makes it difficult for friends, family and casual acquaintances to believe the victim.

Phillip's friends and family would have defended him and would never believe Kasey if she'd confronted them with her reality.

"What? When did that happen?" Carole asked as she grabbed the crudités off a nearby table and offered me some.

"Jeez, he did that months ago. Yup. He opened a separate bank account when he took the job in Albany." I gnawed on a carrot loaded with dip.

"Gee, Kase," Jenny cautioned. "That's not a good sign."

"I've only met him a few times, but he always seemed like such a nice guy," Carole added.

"I know. That's the problem. He is a nice guy. Or at least he can be. None of this adds up," I told them. "That's why I'm convinced he's looking to divorce me, and he's trying to get custody, too."

"Well, I agree he's up to something… but do you really think he wants custody?" Jenny added, frowning.

Under the Microscope:
15 Kasia Delgado, "Is your charismatic partner a secret narcissist? Here's what to look out for," inews.co.uk, April 24, 2024, https://inews.co.uk/inews-lifestyle/love-with-a-narcissist-much-harder-to-leave-them-2988372

CASE FILE 12
Evidence: Minimization and Rationalization

To avoid responsibility, abusers often deny or minimize the consequences of their actions. They deflect the truth and ignore facts to rationalize their thoughts.[16]

In discussing their upcoming wedding, Phillip and Kasey have a massive fight when she suggests an alternative to white napkins.

Phillip is denying reality.

By defending the cost his parents would incur if Kasey wants something other than simple linens, he reinforces his own belief in a different reality and manipulates the situation by presenting his self-serving denials. In doing so, he reshapes his reality to align with the false personas he's projecting as "the good son." He avoids taking responsibility for the situation by crafting an alternative narrative and accusing Kasey of being unreasonable.

It started when I casually said, "I thought it would be nice to have something other than white tablecloths and napkins."

"Well, if that costs more than white linens, forget it. I'm not asking my parents to pay for anything more. You could ask your parents to chip in."

"Sure. I'll call them right now and ask them to pay for part of the wedding they know nothing about. Yeah, that will work, telling them their thirty-three-year-old daughter is getting married to the man she's already married to. Should I send them an invitation to attend the wedding, too? How about my brothers and sisters? Are they all invited?"

"Screw you, Kasey. All I said was I didn't want my parents paying for napkins."

"No, Phillip. You said I should ask my parents to chip in. Do you understand how insulting that is under the circumstances? I can only have a few of my most trusted friends attend our wedding because I know they will keep our secret. I'm not allowed to invite even one relative because that would mean revealing the lie we've been trying to maintain. So, no. This isn't about napkins. It's about you spending thousands of dollars of your parent's money because you don't have the balls to tell them the truth."

Under the Microscope:
16 Dr. George Simon, "Rationalizing Away Wrongdoings," Dr. George Simon's Character Matters, April 6, 2018, https://www.drgeorgesimon.com/rationalizing-away-wrongdoings/

CASE FILE 13
Evidence: Abandonment

Abandonment is a form of emotional abuse. Abusers use threats of abandonment as a means of controlling their partners.[17]

In this passage, Kasey is chatting with Kate about closing the café and leaving Alexandria.

"I know. I ran into four people at the grocery store while buying some cleaning supplies a few days ago. They were gobsmacked I'd closed. I could barely get out the door without sobbing. I don't want to leave."

"I know. Maybe you can work it out and come back?"

"I'd love to, but it might take a while. Phillip's putting me in a very precarious position financially. I've been selling everything I can to make ends meet. He won't contribute anything toward the bills up here now. He claims it's a waste of his money. I'm so broke I wouldn't have gas money to Cobleskill if it wasn't for this catering job. Suddenly, the café, the building, and everything related to Canada is my responsibility."

"Have you pointed out to him that's abandonment?"

"I doubt he sees it that way. Right now, I'm playing nice. Or at least I'm trying to. I don't want him to realize how alarmed I am about what's been going on or that I suspect he's going to try to divorce me. He's had more time to put a plan in place than I have. If we do end up in court, I can show them how I was completely responsible for the Beans and everything else once he moved back to the States."

"Are you sure that's all it is? I know you've told me you hate confronting him."

"You're right, but that's not it. I'm trying to figure out what Phillip's doing before I act. A good friend of mine taught me that."

She smiled and nodded.

Under the Microscope:
17 Dr. Sharie Stines, LPPC, "Emotional Abuse and Threats of Abandonment," Psych Central, December 20, 2017, https://psychcentral.com/pro/recovery-expert/2017/12/emotional-abuse-and- threats-of-abandonment

CASE FILE 14
Evidence: Devalued

Abusers use criticisms and rejection to undermine their victim's self-esteem. They blame or insult their victims and put the victims on the defense.[18]

Below, Phillip tries to undermine Kasey by ignoring her concerns and devaluing her assessment of the situation. Even though he is rarely home to evaluate the situation, he feels he can offer a better explanation for Lucy's behavior. Phillip elevates the sense of his superiority in an effort to control the situation and undermine Kasey's confidence.

Watching the two babies grow and develop simultaneously enabled me to observe their burgeoning personalities. However, I became concerned about other observations. For example, Lucy cried whenever she heard loud noises, even laughter. She seemed to panic when she saw bright lights. She screamed when I put her on the changing table, so I changed her on the floor. Jack exhibited none of these behaviors.

When I tried to discuss these matters with Phillip, his reaction upset me.

"It's in your head, Kasey. They're both fine. You're just a worrier," Phillip told me.

"But when I take them to playgroup, she's not even interested in playing with the other kids," I reported. "She is totally content playing by herself."

"So what? Maybe she doesn't want to play. Did you ever think of that? You create problems to get attention. What's wrong with you?" he fired back.

I couldn't even respond. Phillip came home each night long after the kids were in bed, yet believed he knew better than I did about these matters. I knew I was right, so I kept exploring the issue and ignored him.

At a well-baby visit, I expressed my concerns to our family doctor. After observing her, the doctor too had concerns and suggested getting early intervention to help her. When I told Phillip, he responded with comments that implied I had forced the doctor to draw his conclusions.

Under the Microscope:
18 Sanjana Gupta, "How to Identify and Escape a Narcissistic Abuse Cycle," verywell mind, May 15, 2024 (upd), https://www.verywellmind.com/narcissistic-abuse-cycle-stages-impact-and-coping-6363187

CASE FILE 15
Evidence: Gaslighting

Abusers use blatant untruths in an accusatory manner to try and deny things they have said, done, or promised.[19]

Phillip and Kasey are discussing his lack of doing chores.

"I have stuff to do, so I don't feel like waiting," he told me.

"Well, this is my stuff to do. And while we're on the subject, why is it that when you were home alone, we could afford a housekeeper, but now that I'm home alone with the Beans, that's off the table?"

"What housekeeper?"

"What do you mean, what housekeeper? Have you forgotten about Lynette?"

"No, I haven't forgotten. Look, Kasey. Don't blow this up. I can easily count the number of times Lynette came to clean."

"What are you talking about? She came here once a week for years!"

"I'm not doing this, Kasey. You exaggerate everything."

"How am I exaggerating?"

Soon, the morning turned dark. He ignored my questions, so I pressed because I knew I wasn't the one exaggerating.

"So, she only came occasionally? Really? And was that you who had meals on the table when I came home each night?" I said, becoming impatient. "You spent your time shopping for groceries and doing laundry all those years? Did you empty the litter boxes and pay the bills? You were the one doing that the whole time? Gee, I thought it was me."

"There you go again. You're pretty pathetic. Why is this even an argument? I can't be expected to come home from work and do housework, so forget about Lynette. As it is, I spend all my time working to support you and my family."

"Need I remind you that you only took a few freelance jobs in almost three years before the kids were born? Why was it okay to pay for someone to clean when you were home alone? And secondly, how can you forget I supported you for years?"

> *Phillip is gaslighting Kasey. Abusers knows the truth and they still try to convince their victim that they're mistaken by insisting that despite evidence, the victim is the one who is confused or lying or exaggerating.*
>
> *Even though Kasey knows Phillip is lying and denying the truth her experiences and perceptions, she begins to question her memory and doubt her judgement. Her self-esteem slowly begins to erode even though she has proof she is right. Reality becomes confusing as Phillip's description of events and continuous questioning of her memory begin to traumatize her.*

"Arguments like this persisted. Phillip claimed I exaggerated or outright lied about the past even when I had proof to the contrary. He used a common phrase, "I wish I had recorded what you said because I'd play it back so I could prove you're lying." Or sometimes he claimed, "You don't even hear what you just said."

There were times I started thinking it was all in my head. When he wasn't home, I'd dig through records to prove I wasn't losing my mind. I had canceled checks to show that Lynette came each week, yet his accusations made me question myself, always putting me on the defensive. I began to believe something was wrong with me. I started to think I couldn't trust that the words I thought I spoke were the words that came out of my mouth."

Under the Microscope:
19 Stephanie Moulton Sarkis PhD, *Gaslighting: Recognize Manipulative and Emotionally Abusive People — and Break Free*, (Da Capo Lifelong Books, October 2, 2018)

CASE FILE 16
Evidence: Isolation

Abusers isolate their victims to control their activities and social interactions. By influencing where their victims go and who they communicate with, they reduce a person's access to other people and resources.[20]

Throughout their marriage, Phillip uses many tactics to control Kasey. Now that they would once again be living together, his goal seems to not only be to control their finances, but who she spends time with. By exerting control over her life, he isolates her from any form of a support network that might encourage her to leave him.

A profound loneliness crept into my heart as I headed toward the border. I drove south toward Cobleskill and had hours to think about the future. I was tired of starting over every few years. I longed for a home and a place where I could feel settled. I wanted that place to be Alexandria. At one point, Phillip had wanted that, too. I knew I would make new friends, but the constant upheaval left me feeling defeated.

Knowing that Phillip could soon exert even more control over my life than ever before made me distraught. Even worse, I feared the isolation. The friendships I'd developed in Alexandria had sustained me. However, once I moved to Cobleskill, cultivating new relationships would be a point of contention. Phillip told me the desire for friendships outside our marriage was unnatural. Even before we had children, he constantly discouraged me from socializing. I struggled to understand why. I knew the gathering at Jenny's only happened because he wasn't in Canada.

Under the Microscope:
20 "Social isolation can be domestic violence," DVConnect, (November 1, 2020, https://www.dvconnect.org/social-isolation-can-be-domestic-violence/

CASE FILE 17
Evidence: Intimidation

Abusers use intimidation to instill the fear of harm in their victim. The abuser demonstrates they are capable of violence. They can threaten harm to children, animals or the victim themself. They use intimidation to make victims compliant and force them into submission.[21]

In the passage below, Phillip is angry that Kasey and her neighbor Shannon painted the dining room without his permission.

Phillip uses Kasey's fear of the exposed wiring to intimidate her. While Phillip never expresses the type of violence other abusers exhibit such as physically assaulting their victim, or threatening to, he intimidates her in more subtle ways. Ignoring her concern makes Kasey feel as if she isn't worthy of him wanting her to be safe, especially when he seems pleased that the entire situation makes her nervous.

Anything related to the house was under his complete domain and done at his discretion. Once, when I complained about an unsafe light fixture with exposed wiring right near a shower stall in the bathroom, he scoffed at my concern. It didn't get fixed for years, even though it would have taken less than half an hour. The fact it made me nervous seemed to please him.

I believed Phillip feared that anyone from the outside could weaken his influence over me. While I did have a few friends in Blairstown, somehow, if they didn't meet his approval, socializing with them was a major flash point. It had become so commonplace that I didn't have the perspective necessary to see any of it until I moved to Alexandria, and I no longer needed Phillip's approval.

Under the Microscope:
21 "Domestic Abuse: 5 Control Tactics and How to Counter Them," Healing Well Counseling, https://healingwellcounseling.com/blog/domestic-abuse-5-control-tactics-counter/

CASE FILE 18
Evidence: Lying

Abusers use lying as a tactic to gain power and control over others. Lying not only confuses the victim and those unaware of the lie, but it establishes an alternate reality that allows them to shirk from responsibility. Lying is a form of manipulation of a person or situation.[22]

In the passage below, Phillip announces he has accepted a job back in the States. Phillip lies to shield himself. He manipulates the situation, trying to make it seem as if he's the responsible party by taking the job back in the States. Kasey is disoriented by his confession and distraught that he is abandoning his family in favor of a job that will separate them once again. It becomes clear that all the reasons for moving north were invalid and she will suffer the consequences of his lies.

The altered reality abusers thrust upon their victims is overwhelming. The likelihood that Kasey could achieve the goals originally set out by the two of them as a couple has established a dynamic that can only lead to failure. But Phillip's insistence that he could help long distance negates his family responsibilities as well, leaving him with only a fraction of the tasks they would need to run their business.

"You will never believe who I just got off the phone with!" Phillip told me excitedly.

"Well, I hope it was our lawyer because we still haven't heard back from him," I teased.

"Marco called. He's opening a new company in New Jersey and offered me a job. Isn't that great?"

At that moment, even hearing his old boss's name startled me. It was as if our two worlds had collided, and part of the life we had put behind us seeped through to this new life we were working to create. Knowing Phillip's fondness for working with Marco colored my response.

"That's fantastic! Congrats, honey! He knows you'll have to work remotely, right?"

"Well, not exactly. He wants me to be in the office. I already told him I'd accept the position."

"What?" My jaw hit the floor. "Is he willing to pay for the costs of moving back?"

That's when Phillip told me that none of his former colleagues knew we'd moved to Canada. It was the whole secret marriage situation all over again. I realized Marco had no idea that Phillip had jumped at the opportunity to leave his wife and kids in a foreign country to take a job back in the States. This blew my mind.

"You told me that a restaurant could be a tremendous gamble. I'm nervous that if this doesn't work out, we'll have no income," he maintained. "We're spending a lot to get this going."

"Phillip, I told you that *before* we bought the property. You said we should do it. It was our chance to turn our lives around. We've invested our time and money into opening the business."

"We can still run the business. I can help develop marketing from anywhere, and I'll come home on weekends," he assured me.

My face began to crumble in disbelief at Phillip's assessment of the situation. I squeezed my eyes shut and turned my back, unable to look at him. Leaning against the kitchen counter, I studied the tile pattern, desperate to focus on anything but the words he'd just uttered. He came toward me and gently rubbed the back of my arm. I pulled away and turned to him, trying to find a thread of reason within him.

"So, I'm supposed to stay here, care for the kids, and run a new business on my own? Aren't you the same man who wanted to spend time with his family? Didn't you say you hated missing such a sizable chunk of the Beans' lives? How could you tell him 'yes' without discussing it with me? You get upset if I use the bathroom without telling you that's where I'm going." He stared past me. The pleas in my voice didn't seem to register. "The whole point of moving here was to be together as a family, Phillip. What is the point of doing this if we are not together?"

"I just don't think I should turn down this position. I'll make more than you can make here at the café, and I can still visit. Don't make me feel guilty for wanting to provide for my family, Kasey."

Under the Microscope:
22 "Is Lying Abuse?," The MEND Project, https://themendproject.com/is-lying-abuse/

CASE FILE 19
Evidence: Guilt

Abusers instill guilt and shame by preying upon the insecurities caused by a slowly eroding sense of self-esteem. They make demands of their victims and question their loyalty, making them doubt their self-worth.[23]

Kasey's reactions to Phillip's demands underscore the impact of trauma. She is numb at the thought of living as a friendless stranger in a foreign country and Phillip's lack of concern for her and for their children. Instead of being concerned for the well-being of his family, he tells her it will be her fault if the business is a failure, abdicating all responsibility.

Additionally, the dynamic of this situation created another form of financial abuse. Kasey's time, talent and labor would be exclusively used to start the business they were supposed to operate together.

The day before Phillip left to resume his life back in the States, he said something that, over time, bothered me more and more. The Beans sat at a table in our newly decorated tearoom, eating dessert. While I brought the dirty dishes into the kitchen, Phillip followed me and grabbed me from behind. I spun around so he could hold me. I was utterly despondent over his leaving.

"I'll miss you, you know," he whispered, holding me close.

"Me, too," I said, trying to keep my emotions in check.

"If Marco's company takes off, I'll let you and the Beans move back to the States, I promise," he assured me.

"Why can't we come back now? We still have plenty of money in the bank. I don't want to do this all alone."

"Look, that's not a smart thing to do. This is a new venture, and who knows if it will take off. If it doesn't, we'll be in the same boat without the money to start over again." Then, with little emotion, he added, "Promise me one thing? Don't start making friends here because we need this business to fly, and I know you, you'll end up blowing it because you'll spend time with your new pals."

Caught up in thoughts of him leaving, I never processed what he'd said. Instead, I just nodded and told him, "Sure."

Under the Microscope:
23 Simone Marie, "Why the 'Guilt Trip' Comes Naturally (but Can Be Problematic)," Psych Central, April 27, 2022, https://psychcentral.com/health/guilt-trip

CASE FILE 20
Evidence: Controlling Assets

Abusers restrict the use of joint assets to maintain control over their victims. This is a form of financial abuse.[24]

Having a lack of her own money forces Kasey into the humiliating position of having to provide for herself by any means necessary. Having a cell phone is critical to her safety and well-being, something that Phillip should have considered. However, her needs and those of their children were secondary. Phillip's outburst at the work around shows his true mission is to isolate Kasey by controlling her access to money, even the change she has scraped together. The fact she spent money without his permission infuriates him. This shows the depths of his need to control her every action. His abuse is escalating in the threatening insinuation of "Just wait." While he doesn't touch her physically, the emotional damage is done as Kasey now has to be concerned not only for maintaining her safety while out and about, but from within the home as well.

My next mission was to get a phone. It pissed me off that no one could contact me in the States when Chubby first got lost. Phillip had refused to install a landline at the apartment. He wanted to isolate me again from my friends and family, and I vowed I wasn't going to let it happen anymore.

I dug through every crevice I could in the apartment and van until I had about fifty dollars in quarters, nickels, and dimes. I left the pennies at home and hid them for an emergency. With that, I walked into a local credit union.

"I'd like to open an account," I told the clerk.

"Someone can help you with that in a minute. Have a seat." I felt like I'd asked them to be my co-conspirators in a crime because I had already anticipated a negative reaction from Phillip. I held the bag of change close, embarrassed that my life had come to this.

Later that day

I relished the thought of him reading this email. I'd only been in town for a few days and had already made connections. His email expressed that he was happy they had found Chubby but offered no clue about his feelings regarding the catering job.

After the meeting at school, I called Jenny through the computer to let her know I'd be heading to Canada Friday afternoon. I heard Phillip come in, so I ended my conversation.

"Who were you talking to?" he asked.

"Jenny. I told her the kids and I would fetch Chubby tomorrow. She offered to let us stay with her."

"I thought you couldn't call Canada on your cell?"

"I can, but it eats up my minutes in roaming charges. I ran out of airtime calling Jody, anyway. Besides, I wasn't using my cell. I bought a device for my computer. It's called a magicJack. It works over the Internet.

He went ballistic. Phillip's face turned red, and he left the room. I thought he'd gone to Jack's room to sulk, but moments later, he came back and screamed at me.

"Where did you get the money for that?"

"I used some change."

"What change?"

"It was just loose change I found."

"My change? You're a thief, Kasey!"

"What are you talking about? That's not stealing. I used my loose change and more that I found around the apartment. Most of it was mine, and I had every right to use it."

That wasn't exactly true. I used the change I found in the van, the closet, the mudroom, and other places. But his response indicated that he believed it all belonged to him.

"You're such a liar, Kasey. Just wait."

He stormed off and shut himself in Jack's room. The twins sat on the couch and looked at me when I passed them and pounded on the bedroom door. I wanted to scream at him, but when I saw the look on their faces, I stopped. My need to express my anger wasn't worth putting them through this.

Under the Microscope:
24 "About Financial Abuse," National Network to End Domestic Violence (NNEDV), https://nnedv.org/content/about-financial-abuse/

CASE FILE 21

Evidence: Controlling Employment

Abusers often try to prohibit their partner from working, or sabotage their employment or educational opportunities to prevent them from acquiring the financial resources necessary to become independent. This is a type of financial abuse.[25]

In the passage below, Phillip wants Kasey to contribute to the income but not have enough money to be independent of him. The skills she offers in teaching a film class gives them a financial break, but Phillip disregards this as being a contribution because it isn't something he can control.

"Have you started applying for a real job?" he asked me.

"Are you talking about doing some catering for the school? That is a real job," I retorted.

"No. I mean the film class you offered to teach," he responded.

"Teaching that class will help us financially because we don't have to pay tuition. If it doesn't work out, I'll let it go after a semester."

He rolled his eyes. "Why can't you apply at Walmart? I'm sure they're hiring."

That was Phillip's solution to everything. I'd make more money in one evening as a caterer than in a week at Walmart. It seemed like he wanted me to find work that paid minimum wage so I could contribute to the household income without the ability to do anything more.

Under the Microscope:

25 "Is My Partner Sabotaging My Job? Even from a distance, an abusive partner can undermine you," jbws, https://jbws.org/news/is-my-partner-sabotaging-my-job-even-from-a-distance-an-abusive-partner-can-undermine-you/

CASE FILE 22
Evidence: Blame Shifting

Abusers deflect blame onto their partners to avoid taking any responsibility for their actions or behavior. This perpetuates a cycle of manipulation, control, and emotional abuse.[26]

In the passage below, Kasey replies to Phillip's email request about speaking with "mediators," his sister, Rachel, and Kasey's brother, Jake.

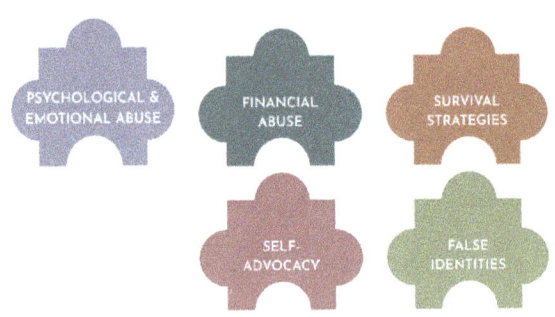

Phillip tries to further control Kasey by enlisting the aid of his sister as his mediator. Rachel knows little about her brother's actions and is also being manipulated. He seeks to validate his belief that Kasey is at fault for all things wrong in their marriage and refuses to consider he has any responsibility for the tensions between them.

"BTW- No. I have not put a list together for our "mediators." I would like to address issues that are important to me without being accused of insinuating things, just like you have here. I want to address the issues that matter TO ME. How do you expect me to detail things that are matters of the heart, that outline the conflicts I have with our relationship, when I can't be assured an email about getting a phone installed isn't going to be blown up? So, no, Phillip. I haven't.

I went to a computer place on Monday. They don't do this repair. They said it doesn't last, and people get angry, so they stopped doing it. Ask the kids. They were with me. They referred me to a place in New Hartford and said I was looking at about $300. If you doubt this, call yourself, and verify."

I provided him with the phone number and address of the computer store and pushed the send button. From that point on, I began to make plans to leave him. I also called Verizon and ordered a telephone.

Under the Microscope:
26 Peg Streep, "5 Kinds of Blame-Shifting, and Why They Work," Psychology Today, February 14, 2023, https://www.psychologytoday.com/us/blog/tech-support/202302/verbal-abusers-and-the-fine-art-of-the-blame-shift

CASE FILE 23

Evidence: Threats

Abusers intentionally instill fear in their victim by making threats. Threats are a form of manipulation and intimidation which impact a victim by employing psychological or emotional distress.[27]

In the passage below, Kasey discusses Phillip's behavior with her new friend.

Phillip shows no regard for his family's safety and is determined to undermine Kasey's right to get the van fixed. His unsettling comments are meant to deter her from acting upon her own instincts. She acknowledges her concern about Phillip's threats, but she chooses to defy him nevertheless because she begins to realize the depth of his disdain.

We spoke over the phone almost daily after she pulled Meg from school. She would tell me about her trials over selling her house, and I would tell her what was happening with Phillip. When I told her about my growing concerns about Phillip's stress levels and the fact that he frequently made unsettling comments, she grew more concerned. One incident in particular rattled her.

It started when I told him I wanted to address the issues with the van. I'd already broken down several times. Fortunately, I was close to Sacred Heart or home each time. But without a cell phone, I was always at risk of being stuck somewhere, with or without the kids.

"We can't afford that right now."

"If you were driving it back and forth to work, it would get fixed. A guy from school owns a repair shop, and I'm calling him to get an appointment. Don't worry. I'll pay for the expense on my own."

"Kasey, first of all, I told you 'no.' Secondly, how will you pay for it on your own?" he asked me mockingly.

"I'll borrow the money or put it on a credit card. Phillip, you may not know this, but I have every right to do this. And guess what? I will. I know you think that just because you're the only one bringing in an income right now, you have the right to dictate everything to me, but you don't. I can and will get the van fixed. And if you don't like it, go screw yourself."

I was so mad that I stormed upstairs, where the Beans were reading, and forgot to bring my laptop.

Under the Microscope:
27 Jonathan Greene, "Research shows link between threats and domestic violence," CNHI News, April 29, 2017, https://www.cnhinews.com/cnhi/article_baed9cf6-2d08-11e7-92ef-f38ef53bd727.html

CASE FILE 24
Evidence: Financial Infidelity

In any relationship, the thoughts, feelings and decisions of both individuals should be taken into account. Not doing so negatively impacts their health and well-being in the dynamics of their relationship and establishes an element of financial infidelity. The abuser's money behaviors cause financial trauma for their victims.[28]

Kasey discusses Phillip's behavior with her new friend Maryanne. Phillip humiliates Kasey by forcing her to ask for money and demanding receipts for any money she spends. The amount of control Phillip exhibits is escalating.

After I got off the phone, I convinced myself I was getting worked up over nothing, and I began to backpedal and soften my concern. Surely, Phillip would never hurt me. Almost every night, Phillip stayed holed up in Jack's room, working on freelance projects, since he'd agreed to do some copywriting for Marco again on the side. He said it was because we needed to bring in extra income. The image of him diligently working to provide for his family erased the one of a raging maniac.

"Do you need the money? Is he telling the truth?" Maryanne asked one day.

"I don't know. I have no idea how much he is making or how the money is being spent. Whenever we need food or something, I have to email him a list, and he goes shopping because he refuses to give me access to much cash or his debit card. Whenever I need gas, I have to ask him for money. And he expects a receipt and change if there is any. I hate the amount of control he's exerting over me financially," I explained.

After I got off the phone, my conversation with Maryanne had me stewing whenever it came to mind. I couldn't help but think of the fact that I never once thought of my hefty agency paychecks as my money versus his money. When I worked in advertising and made a six-figure income, he always had access to every dime I made. Now, the lack of independent resources humiliated me.

Under the Microscope:

28 Julia Kagan, "Financial Infidelity: When Couples Lie to Each Other About Money," Investopedia, June 27, 2024, https://www.investopedia.com/terms/f/financial-infidelity.asp

CASE FILE 25
Evidence: Racking up Debt / Ruining Credit

Abusers can also impact a victim's finances far into the future if they rack up credit card debt or ruin their victim's credit. This makes it harder for the victim to leave, especially if they have no access to, or knowledge of, the financial accounts, or that this activity is happening. This is a form of financial abuse.[29]

Kasey discusses Phillip's behavior with the counselor.

"When we incurred an overdraft fee on our bank account, he claimed I was financially irresponsible. I don't know if he made that up because he was in the States, and all the bank records for that account go to him. But even if I did overdraft the account, he seems to have a convenient memory of the main issues surrounding our finances."

"Give me an example."

"Well, I agreed to move to Canada if he was willing to sell some rental properties we owned. He wanted to finish renovating them before putting them on the market, and I agreed with that. But he ran up our credit cards while I was in Canada. He spent so much money repairing the rental properties we had to file for bankruptcy. Even though I lived hundreds of miles away and the expenses were almost exclusively due to costs related to the repairs on those properties, somehow, he believes I'm the one who is financially irresponsible. I didn't blame him when that went down. He wasn't buying luxury items or anything. I knew he was working hard to finish the renovations. He just invested too much into them before the market fell apart. But now, every dime I spend is scrutinized. He's even told others I am at fault for all our financial problems. He's told me that even getting a phone at the house or a working computer is an unnecessary expense. I have no idea if we can afford these things because he doesn't allow me access to the bank account."

"Has this financial dynamic between you always existed? Has he always taken such a tight rein on the finances?"

"No. When I worked full-time, we had equal access to our funds. Wait a minute. Here's the thing. Phillip doesn't count what he spends on business-related items as personal expenses. So, while operating his film business, he bought whatever equipment he needed, and I had no say. The same thing applies to costs regarding the rental properties.

Under the Microscope:
29 "What is coerced debt?," Surviving Economic Abuse, September 2021, https://survivingeconomicabuse.org/i-need-help/debt/what-is-coerced-debt/

CASE FILE 26
Evidence: Financial Trauma

Abusers use money to exploit their victims. When they require their victim to get permission from them to spend money, or restrict access to bank accounts and shared income, it is financial abuse. It also extends to an abuser giving their victim a limited amount of money or allowance for basic necessities, or requiring all purchases to go through the abuser, thus maintaining power and control over household finances.[30]

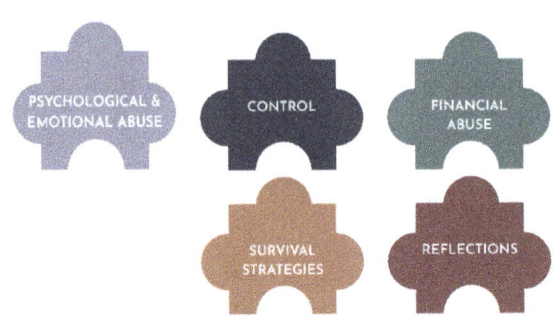

In the passage below, Kasey continues to discuss Phillip's behavior with the counselor.

"It isn't just a money issue. We fight over everything. One day, I moved some furniture around the living room. He was furious with me when he came home. He said since he paid the bills, he had the right to determine the furniture arrangement. I put it back and didn't argue because he's under so much pressure. I'm afraid something will make him snap."

"Why do you think he wants to prevent you from having money?"

"I'm not sure." I stopped to think.

"I think you know why."

"No. I don't understand it. I've never withheld money from him. He seems pleased to have stripped me of my autonomy."

"If you had the financial resources to leave, would you?"

"Yes."

"That's your answer. He's controlling you. All his actions show this is the source of his anger and resentment. Abuse is about power and control."

"I told you he's never laid a hand on me."

"He doesn't need to. Abuse isn't always about violence. When a person is trying to control someone, it often takes the form of emotional abuse or financial abuse. Even gaslighting a partner is a form of abusive behavior, because those are ways someone takes control of another individual. Not all abusers strike their victims. But let me be clear. If he exerts the extent of financial control you describe, that is abuse. He's trying to prevent you from communicating with others by limiting your access to a phone and transportation. Isolating someone is another way to gain control. You pointed out that's something he's done for years."

"I think he's just really stressed about ensuring he's providing for his family, don't you think?"

> *Kasey discusses Phillip's behavior with the counselor.*

"That might be an enormous part, but he's not providing for your emotional well-being. He isn't thinking about that aspect of his behavior. I'm sure much of this is also affecting your twins." The thought made me want to heave.

"Do you think he would change if I found a job?"

"No. I think your husband would find another way to control you."

"But if I found a job, he wouldn't be able to control me, right?"

He glanced up at the clock on the wall. The forty-five minutes had already evaporated.

"What do you think I need to do?" I heard my voice pleading for a resolution to the anguish I felt.

"You need to leave and protect your kids. This is not a safe situation. Would you like to make another appointment?" he asked.

I made an appointment for the following week but never went back.

On the way back to the apartment, everything should have come into focus. In forty-five minutes, the counselor figured out what was right before me, yet I refused to see it. The word *abuse* sounded ridiculous to me. It didn't apply to Phillip.

"His need for control wasn't abuse," I reasoned. It was just the way he dealt with his stress. Neither was his desire for power over me, his dismissive attitude, and his constant humiliation over the simplest things. I assured myself none of that amounted to abuse. I wasn't even sure what the counselor meant by "gaslighting." I looked it up when I got home. I convinced myself that the counselor's assessment was only based on one session, and once we'd talked more, he'd understand I wasn't abused. Phillip and I just had significant marital issues because of difficult circumstances.

Under the Microscope:
30 Joyce Marter, LCPC, "Financial Trauma: Symptoms, Causes, & How to Cope," Choosing Therapy, May 3, 2024, https://www.choosingtherapy.com/financial-trauma/

CASE FILE 27
Evidence: Post-Traumatic Stress Disorder

Abusers can cause post-traumatic stress disorder (PTSD) because victims often relive the traumatic events they cause. Nightmares and flashbacks can occur and  *result in feelings of fear, isolation, irritability and guilt. A person suffering from PTSD may suffer from hypervigilance, have problems sleeping, or find it difficult to focus.*[31]

The passage below takes place after Kasey's visit to the counselor. Phillip's constant threatening actions cause Kasey stress and anxiety. On display is the hypervigilance as she constantly assesses the potential threats of Phillip's words. While PTSD can be caused by a wide variety of incidents, those who have survived abuse often exhibit signs.

In the following days, I grew even more anxious, not knowing what state of anger he would be in whenever he walked through the door. Sometimes, he was genuinely pleasant. But, more often than not, he became tense and irritable when he arrived back in Cobleskill. Sometimes, he seemed like he could snap any minute.

After weeks of trying, I admitted that being on my best behavior didn't help much. Phillip's erratic behavior fed my unease. So much so that one day, I called Phillip at work and asked him to buy a can of wasp spray on his way home. Although he didn't ask why, likely assuming I had discovered an out-of-season nest. I had no intention of using the spray to kill wasps. Instead, I hid the can upstairs next to the bed as protection in case Phillip came at the kids and me in a sudden rage.

Under the Microscope:
31 "Hypervigilance and PTSD," PTSD UK, https://www.ptsduk.org/hypervigilance-and-ptsd/

CASE FILE 28
Evidence: Humiliation

Abusers use humiliation to disorient their victims by degrading them. Verbal assaults such as belittling, ridiculing, or devaluing them has a negative impact on the way the victim perceive themselves.[32]

Phillip consistently tries to prevent Kasey from having access to money which provides her with autonomy.

Having access to my Canadian bank account and the money from the school lunch program provided some relief. Even though I needed to watch every penny, it gave me a level of independence I didn't have when I had to beg Phillip for money. The humiliation I endured every time I handed back the change and receipts from the grocery store or gas station reminded me of how difficult it would be to leave my marriage. Since he refused to share financial information about his new job, I had no idea what child support or alimony would look like. I wrestled with countless questions about how to provide for the Beans and myself once I left. Jobs were still scarce due to the recession, and the low-wage jobs that were available wouldn't cover living expenses. I'd most likely have to rely on welfare, or I shuddered to think we'd become homeless if I dared to leave. I breathed a sigh of relief that, once again, I had even a tiny amount of funds of my own.

Under the Microscope:
32 Neel Burton M.A., M.D., "The Psychology of Humiliation: What is humiliation and can it ever be justified?," Psychology Today, June 23, 2024, https://www.psychologytoday.com/us/blog/hide-and-seek/201408/the-psychology-of-humiliation

CASE FILE 29
Evidence: Gaslighting

Abusers use gaslighting to deny reality or pretend to "forget" what actually occurred. The impact makes the victim question their own thoughts and memorie,s and they can become confused, anxious, isolated, and depressed.[33]

In this passage, Phillip and Kasey argue after he refuses to help the twins with homework and claims he must find a job to support them because the Café isn't earning enough income. Phillip trivialized the work that Kasey did to support them financially for years. He wants her to feel like she is a burden and what she did was unimportant in the context of her financial input and ultimately their marriage.

"You've never worked at anything more than an admin job."

I walked over to the office closet where my café records were stored. While trying to locate something earlier in the week, I found a box of old invoices from my time at one of the ad agencies where I worked before the babies were born. I pulled it out of the closet and threw the papers at Phillip. The bi-weekly invoices were for $5,550.00 each.

"They don't pay a person this much for an admin job, even in Manhattan, Phillip. You can lie to yourself, but I have the physical proof here."

He wouldn't look at them. It was all right there in black and white, yet he denied it.

Under the microscope:
33 Stacey Benson, "Gaslighting – When Abusers Distort Reality," Jeff Anderson and Associates, PA, December 16, 2023, https://www.andersonadvocates.com/blog/gaslighting-when-abusers-distort-reality/

CASE FILE 30
Evidence: Financial Sabotage

Abusers sabotage their victim's earning potential as a way to prevent them from becoming independent. This is a form of financial abuse.[34]

In this passage, Phillip insists he have access to the Café kitchen right before the lunch rush so he can prepare his own meal, suggesting the Café food is not suitable.

Access to money provides autonomy. Although Phillip wanted the Café to succeed in some ways, he also needed Kasey to fail to prove his point.

Philip knew I wouldn't say anything in front of my employees and customers. He relished inserting himself into our daily routine and showing Kate and Sharilyn that he, too, was their boss. He didn't care that this also made a statement about the food quality at the café. Soup was our specialty. I had customers drive all the way from Montreal, which was an hour away, to have a bowl of our soup.

When we closed that day, I told Kate and Sharilyn I would finish up because, by then, I was seething. I climbed the stairs and let Phillip have it.

"What do you think you were doing with your little stunt this morning? It's not enough that you refuse to help me, but now you want to sabotage my business?"

"That's just it, Kasey. This is your business. It's always about you and what you want."

"What do I want? Do you think this is about what I want? You were the one who wanted to move here. Did you think I would just step aside because you're here now?

"I wanted some lunch. Was that too much to ask? Are you saying I can't even use the kitchen for a few minutes?"

"Did it ever occur to you that we have a kitchen in our apartment? This had nothing to do with you wanting lunch, Phillip. You wanted to show who is in charge." I left him, slamming the office door shut, and, as usual, we didn't talk for days. After that, he spent even more of his time in the office.

Under the Microscope:
34 Sarah Gonzalez Bocinski, "Unable to Leave: Economic Sabotage and Exploitation in Abusive Relationships," Futures Without Violence, October 25, 2018, https://www.futureswithoutviolence.org/unable-leave-economic-sabotage-exploitation-abusive-relationships/

CASE FILE 31
Evidence: Emotional Abuse

An abuser's behavior is motivated by their desire for power and control over their victim. They will use various tactics to manipulate the victim's emotions. While emotional abuse is harder to identify, the trauma is very real, as the victim is made to feel ashamed, guilty, violated, erased, or silenced into compliance.[35]

In the passage below, Kasey notifies Phillip her father has died, and his lack of an appropriate response leaves her numb.

Phillip is being emotionally abusive to Kasey by denying her the right to grieve for her father. In dismissing her feelings, he shows his indifference and even ties the issue to the Café and the need to stay open, rather than agreeing to close for the day as Kasey requested.

Phillip shows more concern for the cost of paying for employees than he does for his wife's sorrow. He is displaying another tactic of financial abuse in so much that abusers insist the victim work for no wages in a family business.

Phillip was up in the office. I trudged upstairs and delivered the news, ignoring the glow of the TV monitor. I told Phillip my dad had passed.

"That's too bad," he said, returning to watching one of his favorite sci-fi shows.

The callousness of his comment left me unable to move. He never cared for my father, and I understood he had reasons. The moment shouldn't have been about how he felt about my father but about the loss I was experiencing. What he said reminded me of how often this scene had played out in small ways throughout my marriage. Whenever I showed even the slightest emotion or feeling, he invalidated it. I couldn't possibly be hungry if he wasn't hungry. I couldn't possibly be in pain if he wasn't in pain. He shut me down as if anything I experienced wasn't real because it wasn't happening to him. The magnitude of my father's death finally made me see Phillip's actions and reactions for what they were. He did try to control, dominate, and degrade me. He distorted my reality because nothing anyone experienced was real if it wasn't about him. I turned and rushed downstairs without further comment. He came down moments later and found me in the kitchen crying.

"Should we send flowers?" he asked.

I turned to him, exasperated. "Who would you send flowers to? My brother Ray?" I asked.

"I don't know. I'm trying to help," Phillip said sharply.

"I'm calling Sharilyn and Kate to let them know I need to close the café tomorrow," I said, then headed upstairs to use the phone in our apartment.

"You can't do that! We can't risk losing that business," he yelled as I crossed the room.

"We," I thought bitterly. There was never a 'we' in running the café.

I crossed the tearoom and opened the door connected to the foyer to make my way upstairs to our tiny apartment above. Phillip followed me. When I reached the bottom of the staircase, he grabbed the back of my arm and stopped me before I climbed it. I threw his hand off my arm and faced him.

"This is what it means to have a business," he ranted. "You don't get to close up shop because something happens." It was as if I said I was closing to have my nails done or spending the day at the spa. In the three-plus years we owned the place, I rarely took time off, missing many holidays or special occasions with family and friends. He even threw a tantrum when I wanted to attend Jenny's sixtieth birthday celebration, so I didn't go.

"I'm going to call them to cover for me or close for the day," I said bitterly.

"We can't afford it," he replied to my back as I walked up the stairs.

I turned back to look at him. "Of course not. It doesn't matter, because it's my family. If this were your father, you would have been heading home within minutes of getting the call." I continued into the apartment and locked the door behind me. I couldn't fathom what had just happened.

Under the Microscope:

35 "Hidden epidemic: financial abuse in small and family businesses," Small Business Connections, December 4, 2023, https://smallbusinessconnections.com.au/hidden-epidemic-financial-abuse-in-small-and-family-businesses/

CASE FILE 32
Evidence: Victim Blaming

Abusers will refuse to take responsibility for their actions and often blame the person they are abusing for their actions. Outside observers of a situation where the victim remains in an abusive household make assumptions about why the victim stays in the relationship. They use phrases like "it takes two" to suggest the victim has done something to provoke the abuser, justifying the abuser's actions.[36]

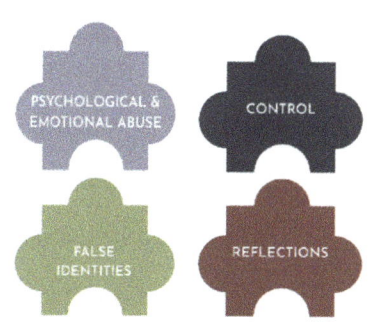

In the passage below, Kasey reflects on when her understanding of what domestic abuse is formed. She was twelve, and learned her neighbor, Mrs. White, was being beaten by her husband each night.

Kasey now realizes that a lack of knowledge leads others to blame the victim for staying in abusive relationships.

When my mother found out her new friend's husband beat her nightly, she was outraged. She confronted my father, who told her it was none of our business. My mother disagreed.

"We should do something!" she told him.

Once I learned the truth, the purple welts I saw on Mrs. White's arms and face sickened me. But at twelve years old, I didn't understand the whole dynamic of the situation and simply wondered why Mrs. White chose to stay with her husband, since I believed she could just take her five children and leave.

Under the Microscope:
36 "Understanding victim blaming and why it's harmful to survivors," Welsh Women's Aid, May 22, 2023, https://welshwomensaid.org.uk/news/understanding-victim-blaming-and-why-its-harmful-to-survivors/

CASE FILE 33
Evidence: Obstacles

In addition to the barriers abusers create for their victims, they also face a multitude of layers when leaving a domestically abusive relationship. Obstacles include concerns for the safety of children, pets and other family members, finding transitional housing, a lack of financial resources, or negative experiences in the past that cause fear of making matters worse when they've suffered retribution or the humiliation of a failed escape attempt.[37]

Kasey faces a complex combination of reasons for fearing her decision to leave. Despite the desire to rid herself of the pain and humiliation of Phillip's actions, her low self-esteem and trauma related thinking made making rational decisions more difficult.

I tried to figure out how to leave safely without Philip gaining knowledge of my plans. I wanted to avoid incurring his wrath so the Beans would be spared the ugliness of yet more fighting. We would need a place to stay until I found work, so I reached out to my brother Jake and was very candid about the state of my marriage and my plans to leave Phillip. He discussed it with Meredith, and they agreed to let us come.

Because one of the tenants in Alexandria emailed me about a problem with her water heater, I told Philip that was the main reason for a trip north. That was partially true. I informed him that once the plumber resolved the issue, I planned to head to Vermont to spend time with my brother on the first anniversary of my father's death. That was also partly true. Phillip questioned nothing.

I recognized that the pain of ending our relationship would affect both of us emotionally. I cared about his well-being. I even admitted to myself that, to a great extent, I still loved him very much. Leaving him wasn't about love. It wasn't about getting even or seeking revenge, either. I honestly had no desire to hurt him or cause any needless suffering. The heartache of knowing how little he thought of me weighed heavily into my decision. He never seemed to appreciate my contributions to his life and our marriage. I couldn't understand how he was able to dismiss all of the years I supported him for a version of our lives where he single-handedly played the role of sole provider. Instead, he tried to convince me these were figments of my imagination. There were days I sought out physical reminders of the truth because he got into my head in a way that caused me to doubt myself again.

Under the Microscope:
37 "Barriers to Leaving, Part 1," domesticshelters.org, January 1, 2016, https://www.domesticshelters.org/articles/escaping-violence/barriers-to-leaving-part-i

CASE FILE 34
Evidence: Minimizing

Abusers impact a victim's self-esteem by dismissing, ignoring, or refuting their thoughts, feelings and experiences. A victim's perspective is undervalued and unimportant, thereby impacting their self-confidence. Victims feel insignificant and their personalities erased when their abuser minimizes a victim's pain and suffering.[38]

In the passage below, Phillip emails Kasey after he realizes she has left him.

Despite the fact Phillip and Kasey's marriage has been dysfunctional for years, Phillip believes that all their problems can be resolved in one day. This indicates his complete lack of any understanding of the damage his actions cause. He doesn't offer Kasey solace. He tells her he wants his wife and kids and nothing else is important to him. He unwittingly has stated the obvious. Nothing matters except what he wants.

I would like to resolve things today. You don't have to come up with a list as we had discussed. We can either have Jake and Rachel discuss things, or we can talk directly.

Regardless of how and where this anger between us has come from, I want it over. I heard our new neighbor and her husband (boyfriend?) laughing with their children tonight and they seemed so happy to be together. Here they were, moving into a crummy little apartment and they were so full of joy to just be together. I broke down and cried for a long time.

I want my wife, and I want my kids. Nothing else is more important to me. Let me know how you want this to proceed.

I do love you. I always have and always will.

~ Phillip

Under the Microscope:
38 "When 'Belittling' Crosses the Line into Emotional Abuse," The MEND Project, https://themendproject.com/belittling-in-a-relationship/

CASE FILE 35
Evidence: The Good Guy Behavior

Abusers can turn on the charm at will. When they are convinced it will benefit them, there are times when they return to the good behavior that attracted the victim in the first place.[39]

In the passage below, Kasey reflects on the changes in Phillip's behavior after she and the twins return to Cobleskill. Despite acting as if he has changed, the financial control Phillip continues to exert shows that nothing has changed at all.

Over the next few months, I noticed a significant change in Phillip's behavior. I was cautious, however, because this had happened before. I wanted to believe him, but I couldn't. I'd been through these reprieves too often to trust it would last. I welcomed the calm, but continued to expect the storm. During this time, I found myself still in defensive mode. I tried to pull back, but part of this was because Phillip remained adamant about having me report every penny I spent. Even if he wasn't combative about it, I found it humiliating.

His habit of closing himself off in Jack's room each night didn't change. He was still very private about conversations that I imagined were about something he wanted to keep from me. So even though he tried harder than ever to temper his frustrations when he spoke to the twins and me, I wasn't convinced that anything had changed. I just couldn't do anything about it without money. Phillip still exerted control over all our finances. He still kept his salary and income a secret. But since he wasn't ranting or threatening, I focused more on getting a job since that was the only way I could ever regain my independence if things got ugly again.

It wasn't easy putting a resumé together because my work experience was all over the place. Since I left the advertising industry, I have built websites, got my realtor's license, and taught school. I also worked as a mobile notary, did graphic design, and owned and operated the café. Finding a well- paying job after I'd been out of the regular workforce for years would be challenging. I was also middle-aged and looking for work in a recovering economy. I briefly explored the idea of opening another café or catering business before realizing it couldn't happen without money, and I had none.

Under the Microscope:
39 Lundy Bancroft, *Why Does He Do That?: Inside the Minds of Angry and Controlling Men* (Berkley Books; Reprint edition, September 2, 2003)

CASE FILE 36
Evidence: Dominance Hierarchies

Abusers construct a dominance hierarchy based on the status within a relationship they believe is important. The hierarchy is not always consistent, which disorients the victim. The abuser's actions indicate whether they believe a person is above or below them in status.[40]

In the passage below, Kasey reflects on how Phillip responds to the death of his uncle compared to the death of her father.

From the very beginning of their relationship, Phillip creates a dominance hierarchy between himself and Kasey. His wants and needs come first in all ways.

His inherent belief that his needs are dominant to Kasey's reinforces the notion that he is superior to her, and he exploits his position within the hierarchy to his advantage.

These moments alone caused me to think about feelings I'd managed to shove aside for a while. Phillip's absence began to resurrect my resentment. When my father died, I was discouraged from taking time off to grieve. Yet he left for an entire weekend to attend his uncle's funeral. The matter underscored the continued hierarchy in our relationship. I didn't resent him for going to his uncle's funeral. I resented that Phillip felt he had the right to determine if I could go to my father's. I began to think again about our marriage. I realized the only difference between now and November was that we acted more civil toward one another. I avoided wondering where it would all lead so I could enjoy my time with the Beans.

Under the Microscope:
40 Elinor Greenberg Ph.D., "How Hierarchical Thinking Relates to Narcissistic Abuse," Psychology Today, June 19, 2021,
https://www.psychologytoday.com/us/blog/understanding-narcissism/202106/how-hierarchical-thinking-relates-narcissistic-abuse

CASE FILE 37
Evidence: Withholding Money

When an abuser withholds money, it creates a feeling of instability and makes the victim economically dependent upon their abuser. By limiting access to money and the things that  *money can buy, the victim's self-esteem is damaged, and it becomes more difficult to leave an abuser and access safety. This is a form of financial abuse.*[41]

In the passage below, Kasey responds to the news that she has been offered a job as a sous chef.

The call was from the human resources department at the resort I'd applied to, offering me a position as a sous chef in one of their many kitchens. We discussed some dates for training. I related that I could confirm my availability once I had a chance to discuss my proposed training schedule with Phillip.

It was hard to contain my excitement. By now, I'd become used to asking Phillip to purchase food. But when I needed him to pick up personal hygiene products, it wasn't just uncomfortable; I was embarrassed. Explaining why I still needed sanitary pads or what kind of deodorant I preferred degraded me. When he shopped, he bought any item on sale and claimed I was ungrateful if I made the slightest complaint. Sometimes, he couldn't find time to go to the store, and I had to beg him for money so I could go on my own. He usually resisted and told me I could wait, but if he relented, I was still expected to provide receipts and return the change. This job was a huge step in having a sense of security and confidence I could provide for myself and the Beans. I beamed as I returned to the living room to return the portable phone to the charger.

Under the Microscope:
41 Rachael Pace, "10 Signs of Financial Abuse in Marriage," Marriage.com, June 6, 2023, https://www.marriage.com/advice/finance/financial-abuse-in-a-marriage-what-you-need-to-know-and-do/

CASE FILE 38
Evidence: Transactional Manipulation

When an abuser gives something, they always expect to get something in return, making almost every interaction with them transactional. While some transactional relationships are healthy, it becomes a problem when manipulation is involved and the abuser only thinks in terms of what they will get in return for their cooperation.[42]

In the passage below, Kasey reflects on her relationship with Phillip and how he always wanted something in return for his cooperation.

Phillip devalues Kasey's actions, which impacts her sense of self. By always requiring something in return for his cooperation, he manipulates her emotions, creating a barrier to expressing her needs and willingness to ask for help when it is needed.

I began to justify my thoughts with the recollections of the countless times I was hurt, ill, or emotionally bereft, and Phillip would not offer me an ounce of compassion or sympathy. Even if I'd just spent days nursing him back to health, if I came down with the same cold or flu, anything Phillip did to help me was done begrudgingly.

Almost more annoying was his need for one-upmanship whenever one of us was sick. If I had a headache, he had a migraine. If I had a cold, he had the flu. When I was diagnosed with carpal tunnel and needed surgery, he began wearing a wrist and hand brace, too. Even after the diagnosis and surgery were performed to remove the tumors on my parathyroid glands, he continued to insinuate my claims of exhaustion were just an excuse for tasks left undone and said I was just lazy. It was as if the surgery corrected the problem, and I automatically recovered the following day. The concept of healing seemed to be beyond his grasp.

However, this wasn't just in moments of illness. When I needed a "favor" from him, Phillip would ask, "What will you give me for it?" While his words were always framed as a joke, he was serious. He only seemed willing to do something for me if he would benefit from whatever I asked him to do or if I offered something in return.

Under the Microscope:
42 Kendra Cherry, MSEd, "Transactional Relationships: The Link Between Reciprocity and Connection," verywell mind, February 24, 2024, https://www.verywellmind.com/transactional-relationships-8580613

CASE FILE 39
Evidence: Financial Gatekeeping

Gatekeeping is the act of trying to control who gets certain resources. In the case of financial gatekeeping, those resources are monetary resources. Sometimes this can involve keeping a partner out of what should be shared decisions  *about joint finances. In the case outlined below, it is about controlling access to finances after death. In both instances, it illustrates the abusers need for control and their demonstrative distrust of their victim. Gatekeeping can also extend to times when an abuser makes all the decisions with little to no input from their partner. That is financial gatekeeping.*[43]

In the passage below, Kasey expresses her deep concerns over the lack of money currently, and in the future should something happen to Philip. Kasey's lack of financial independence has brought into focus the insidious nature of financial abuse. Phillip's need for power and control within their relationship extends not only to harming the target of his abuse, Kasey, but his children also witness the abuse and suffer the consequences of his actions well into the future.

I told the social worker I didn't know how we would survive financially, as Phillip would get his last paycheck at the end of April. Our financial realities were bleak, since we canceled our life insurance policies when Phillip lost his job in 2005. He balked at taking out new policies when things got more financially stable.

"I don't want you profiting from my death," he joked.

I didn't find it funny back then, and I certainly resented that decision now. But there was no way I could go back and change things, so I had to live with the knowledge that I was facing some real financial difficulties even if I sold the building in Canada.

In this passage, Phillip is in the hospital with a kidney stone.

"Have you designated a healthcare proxy? We need to make sure everything is in order," the doctor told him. Phillip nodded.

Moments later, a nurse entered the room with papers for Phillip to sign. He read them, filled out the appropriate information, and signed them as routinely as he signed dozens of other documents.

While waiting for the doctor to return, he said, "Just so you know, I've made Rachel my healthcare proxy. The last thing I want is to have you be in charge of pulling the plug," he told me matter-of-factly.

I turned and looked at him, my mouth agape. I couldn't respond. I felt a chill, even though it was the middle of June. I clutched my purse closer to me, then glanced at the floor, determined not to cry. When I finally composed myself, I told him, "Whatever you want is fine." And it was.

They whisked him off for some tests and determined he had a kidney stone, and it had passed. I didn't see him again until they were ready to discharge him.

A palpable silence existed on the ride back to his sister's. After arriving home in Marblehead, we both went to bed without saying goodnight. I climbed into the bed I shared with Lucy, trying not to wake her. Sleep eluded me for much of the night. I couldn't understand how Phillip could be so callous. Then I realized that, in many ways, he had done me a huge favor. By choosing Rachel as his healthcare proxy, Phillip let me know where I stood in our relationship.

Phillip's love was conditional and always had been. When he needed me, I was of value to him. When he didn't require my help, I didn't matter. When Phillip signed that paper earlier, it revealed something I had long suspected but couldn't admit to myself about my role in his life. It wasn't flattering.

The words, "The last thing I want is to have you be in charge of pulling the plug," echoed in my brain. At first, I blamed it on the impact of leaving Phillip eight months earlier. However, looking back, I realized he had made equally damning statements before that when he said things like, "I don't want you profiting from my death." Whatever his reasons were, his concern about my receiving money as a beneficiary of his life insurance obscured his concern to provide for his wife and children. Those were things he said long before I left him.

That night, I tried to reconcile that, for whatever reason, Phillip believed I was unworthy of his trust, protection, loyalty, or commitment to our marriage. I knew I should have realized long ago when he refused to tell his parents we got married. However, that night, I finally understood that his words and actions were more of a statement about his character than mine. I may have loved him imperfectly, but I loved him.

I lay there, wondering if maybe he floated in and out of being in love with me all those years. Loving someone and being in love with them were separate matters

That night, I tried to reconcile that, for whatever reason, Phillip believed I was unworthy of his trust, protection, loyalty, or commitment to our marriage. I knew I should have realized long ago when he refused to tell his parents we got married. However, that night, I finally understood that his words and actions were more of a statement about his character than mine. I may have loved him imperfectly, but I loved him.

Under the Microscope:
43 Bree Rody, "How You Can End Up in a Financially Abusive Relationship Without Even Realizing It," The Financial Diet, March 4, 2020, https://thefinancialdiet.com/how-you-can-end-up-in-a-financially-abusive-relationship-without-even-realizing-it/

CASE FILE 40
Evidence: Minimizing Feelings

When an abuser minimizes or invalidates the victim's feelings, they are belittling the victim's perspective of events. This can look like dismissing, ignoring, or downplay their thoughts, feelings and experiences. This is done as a way of making the victim feel unimportant and lose confidence. It helps the abuser maintain their control and keeps the victim from speaking up about the abuse.[44]

I wondered if he even thought about this milestone, considering the fragility of our relationship. A sense of grief crept over me. I grieved for what I thought we once had together. I grieved because I knew his days were numbered, and there wasn't anything I could do that would ultimately prolong his life. I grieved because he couldn't understand that I had a right to grieve.

"You're not the one who has cancer," he told me again and again.

We were downstairs in Rachel and Dennis's basement when he spoke those words. I had entered the room where Jack and Lucy were sitting with him, reading. I asked if they would walk Chubby, and they readily agreed. When they left, I turned to Phillip.

"I'm leaving for Alexandria early in the morning. Amelia emailed and said she has no hot water again, so, on top of cleaning out the rear apartment, I'll have to get a hold of the plumber." When he said nothing, I tried to fill in the awkwardness. "I wish I didn't have to go north."

"Well, I can't go," he said with a tone of sheer contempt. "Phillip, I'm not suggesting you can. Don't be like that, please."

"Be like what, Kasey? You don't understand what this is like because you don't have cancer. You're going to be seeing your friends while you're up there. Don't lie."

I was tired of holding my tongue. I realized Phillip was suffering, but I was compelled to say something.

"Does your mother and father or Rachel have cancer?" "What are you talking about?"

"You constantly tell me I can't possibly be suffering because I don't have cancer. And yet, you understand they're suffering because of your illness. How is it that you think I've escaped the pain of this?"

He looked at me with disdain. I wasn't arguing or emotional. I presented him with a valid statement. He pursed his lips and seemed about to object, but then he refused to comment.

"Just because I don't have cancer, Phillip, doesn't mean it doesn't affect me. It affects me in ways you refuse to recognize. You recognize their pain and suffering, but somehow, you think I'm immune. That's sad." With that, I left him alone and went upstairs.

Under the Microscope:
44 Darlene Lancer, JD, LMFT, "Forms of Emotional and Verbal Abuse You May Be Overlooking," Psychology Today, April 3, 2017,
https://www.psychologytoday.com/us/blog/toxic-relationships/201704/forms-emotional-and-verbal-abuse-you-may-be-overlooking

CASE FILE 41
Evidence: Subjugation

In situations of coercive control, abusers slowly break down the self-esteem of the victim. They will subjugate them until their victim willingly puts the abuser before their own needs in all situations, caring for them at the detriment of themselves. This tends to be a slow process and one that is often not even realized by the victim until after they are subjugated for a prolonged period of time.[45]

I sat on the couch in Rachel and Dennis's living room, reading the book's last chapters. I knew I should be addressing my own needs, but I struggled since Phillip's needs were the priority. It wasn't something that just happened because he had cancer, either. It reminded me that, as a child, I watched my mother always put her family's needs, especially my father's, before her own. That expectation was cemented long ago. As a woman, I, too, sacrificed my own needs for my family.

I looked over at the Beans, watching a movie as I read. It seemed like an impossible situation. Here, I'd just finished reading a book about self-empowerment. Servan-Schreiber observed that lifestyle changes can fight cancer. Yet, the needs of others drove my lifestyle. Servan-Schreiber's book outlined some fundamental reasons that nutrition, exercise, psychology, and meditation were essential to a person's well-being. However, I was constantly stressed, ate poorly, didn't exercise, or do anything else he recommended in the book. Regardless of what was going on in my life, I had to do better. I finally understood that taking care of myself was taking care of my family.

Under the Microscope:
45 Dr. Emma Katz, "Explaining Coercive Control to People Who Don't Quite Get It: A Series," Decoding Coercive Control with Dr Emma Katz, January 9, 2023, https://dremmakatz.substack.com/p/explaining-coercive-control-to-people

CASE FILE 42
Evidence: The Two Faces of Narcissists

Narcissists often behave like they're two very different people. Their public face is lovable, kind, and charismatic. Often, they are well-known in their communities and loved. Their private face is controlling, sometimes cruel, with hair-trigger mood changes. This does even more to throw off the victim, further forcing them to distrust their own understanding of reality. The abuser's external behavior is a shield behind which the abuser hides, protecting them from any accusations that may arise.[46]

FALSE IDENTITIES

At the doctor's office one day, another pattern emerged. When we were in the company of others, Phillip always presented me as a saint.

"You wouldn't believe what an excellent cook she is!" he told Emma, his nurse, at one visit. "The other night, she made me a delicious soup. I loved it so much, I had three bowls," he continued. "When we owned our restaurant, customers came all the way from Montreal for her cooking," he bragged.

"I didn't know you guys had a restaurant," Emma responded.

"Oh, yes," Phillip told her. "For years. We owned a small café, but we did a lot of catering and other things on the side. We even rented an old barn and hosted a music festival." As Phillip chatted with Emma and described the café and our time in Canada in such glowing terms, I simmered because it occurred to me how often he did this. To others, he offered a totally different view of circumstances than he had presented to me. I wasn't sure which portrayal was the more accurate one. Was he proud of the café and the music festival, or were they the massive failures he told me they were?

On the ride back to Marblehead, I thought about this and understood the significance of his conflicting presentation of situations. He didn't want to portray me negatively in front of others because, to Phillip, that would reflect poorly on him. By praising me, he actually praised himself.

Realizing that Phillip kept his admonishments out of the earshot of others offered me a way to circumvent his callous words. I began avoiding being alone with him whenever possible. I would leave the room, or take the dog for a walk, or just pretend I wanted to use the bathroom. I used this excuse so often that I thought he might begin to think I had a bladder infection.

Under the Microscope:
46 Olivia Guy-Evans, MSc, "What Are The Signs Of A Covert Narcissist? How to Respond, Simply Psychology, November 24, 2023,
https://www.simplypsychology.org/covert-narcissism.html

CASE FILE 43

Evidence: Technology-Assisted Domestic Abuse

Phones and other electronics can either be a tremendous help for abuse victims, or a detrimental harm. Abusers can track internet usage and can restrict access to computers and phones to maintain control over their victims. This is a form of coercive control. In the case shown below, this removal of the victim's access 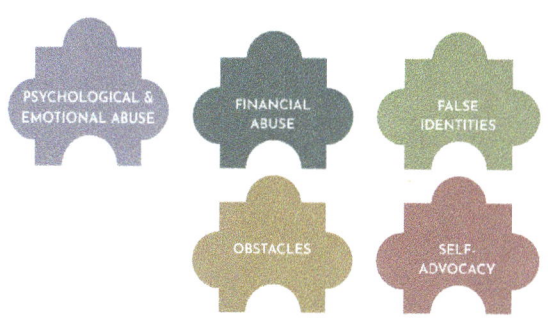 to her cell phone is not only used to isolate and control the victim, but it also endangers the victim as she is driving a great distance with a car that is greatly damaged. The abuser's self-centered behavior leaves the victim without a way to reach anyone if she is stranded on the road. It shows how little he actually cares about his wife.[47]

My plan didn't work out all the time. At the end of July, my brother-in-law Dennis told me that I had racked up their cell phone bill with roaming charges the previous time I'd traveled to Canada. I had no idea that could happen, and I apologized and told him I would compensate him for the expense. Despite this, Phillip ambushed me when I went downstairs to grab Chubby's leash.

"We need to talk right now," he told me from his room. "What's up?" I asked him, trying to sound casual.

"When you go to Canada this week, you have to leave the cell phone in Marblehead, Kasey. I spoke to Dennis and promised him I'd have you give it back to me. He said he couldn't believe how irresponsible you are sometimes."

"Did he?"

"Yeah, he did."

"I've already apologized to Dennis. I didn't realize that I'd get roaming charges when I was in Canada. So, yes, I racked up a hefty bill. But I promised to give him money to cover the additional expense."

"Whatever your excuse, I want it back," Phillip insisted.

"So, you're telling me I shouldn't bring it while I'm traveling?" I asked him incredulously. "It's not yours. Dennis gave it to me. Why you ended up with it is a mystery to me."

"Mystery? I took it initially because you handed it to me and asked me to hold on to it. I kept it on me because we don't have a cell phone of our own."

"This is so typical of you. You ran up an enormous bill, and now you're offering excuses."

"Oh, it's an excuse to want to have a cellphone on me while I'm the one who travels all over the place in a van that shouldn't even be on the road?"

"Don't tell me all those calls were made because of your traveling. That's a load of shit. You use it to call your friends, too."

"Yes, I call my friends. I call my family, too. But you're making it sound like I intentionally ran up the bill. You're the one that's blowing this up."

"I'm always the bad guy for pointing out how irresponsible you are. This is what you do to me. You make me out to be the villain. You have to go there despite everything I'm going through."

I left the room and grabbed Dennis's cell phone from my purse.

"Here. I won't use it anymore. I'm sorry I used it in the first place. I'm even sorrier that you have so little concern for my safety." I grabbed Chubby's leash, stormed upstairs, and took him out for a walk.

Under the Microscope:
47 Bridget Harris, *Technology and Domestic and Family Violence (Routledge Studies in Crime and Society)* (Routledge; 1st edition, January 30, 2023)

CASE FILE 44
Evidence: Insults

Abusers often use verbal insults to belittle their victims. This is another method that is employed to chip away at the self-esteem of the victim. Eventually, the victim begins to believe the cruel things being said about them, and it makes it easier for the abuser to continue bringing their victim down.[48]

Later that day, Phillip and I took the kids to the fencing lessons I worked out for them. I'd completely forgotten to tell him about my conversation with Rachel until we sat in the car chatting with the Beans. I turned to him and said, "Honey, I forgot to tell you, your sister said her friend Laura might be willing to rent us her house."

"What? We can't afford to rent a house."

"We don't know that we can't afford it because we don't know if she's willing to rent it. We can't stay with Rachel and Dennis forever," I joked.

"This is so typical of you. I'm always the last to find out."

"What are you finding out? Nothing has been done. I am relating a conversation Rachel and I had before leaving the house."

"You can't even understand simple math. We can't afford to rent a house," he screamed at me.

"Phillip, calm down. I never said we were renting a house. Rachel brought this up earlier. Now, I'm telling you about our conversation, that's all."

"You lie about everything," he screamed.

The entire argument came out of nowhere, and at that point he was screaming so loud, Lucy and Jack were crying in the back seat. I believed the suddenly explosive conversation was over when Phillip said, "Don't blame this on Rachel. You never take responsibility for anything. You know you're going to hell for all the horrible things you've done to me."

I lost it. "Oh, yeah? Just wait until we get back. Ask your sister who initiated the conversation. You're way out of line, and I'll prove it, not that it matters to you." I screamed at him.

The level of my rage at him surprised us both. The frustration of his unfounded accusation had me so angry, I couldn't contain myself. He got out of the car as if I were going to strike him and called Jack and Lucy to go with him. They reluctantly followed. If he wanted me to display my worst instincts, I didn't disappoint him. When I realized I'd played right into his hand, I was mortified that I'd lost control and began to cry.

> *This passage is after the couple returned to Rachel's house, Rachel mentions the house situation to Phillip.*

"Rachel, Phillip thinks I started this conversation," I said, feeling a bit self-righteous.

She made it clear to him that she brought up the subject. She looked at me as if to question why this was so important, but I didn't offer any additional explanation.

"Well, we'll have to think about it," Phillip told her as he disappeared into the kitchen for some reason.

I didn't wait for an apology because I knew one wasn't coming. When I was cold to Phillip later, he told me to "grow up and get over it." His words could still cut through me, and they were almost too much to bear. If I argued or fought with him, I risked doing more harm to him physically and emotionally, and if I kept it bottled inside, I was harming myself.

I told myself daily that I was not the person he portrayed me to be. I continued to reread emails like Sondra's and Andy's. I retreated into hot showers and went on more long walks with the kids and the dog. I got out of his way whenever I could. He kept telling his friends he was doing his best to survive. I wanted to say to him, so was I.

Under the Microscope:
48 Kristen, "Forms of Verbal Abuse: Insults and Their Delivery," HealthyPlace, November 22, 2018,
https://www.healthyplace.com/blogs/verbalabuseinrelationships/2018/11/forms-of-verbal-abuse-insults-and-their-delivery

CASE FILE 45

Evidence: Power Imbalance

At the root of most abusive relationships, there is a perceived imbalance of power. Maybe one partner makes more money than the other. Maybe one person is more intelligent. Maybe one is older. Maybe one is more beloved in the community. When these perceived imbalances are exploited and manipulated to control the person considered to be the less powerful one, this creates the abusive portion of the relationship. Power imbalances do not necessarily make a relationship abusive, but the exploitation of an imbalance does.[48]

Phillip and I started out with some heavy baggage early on. Because we were often happy in those earlier years, it was difficult to see how much those issues infiltrated and shaped our relationship. Until I began to look back, I couldn't see how detrimental the lie about our first wedding was to our relationship. It had set the stage for future events and became the catalyst for the imbalance of power that drove a wedge between us.

I looked across the room where Phillip lay sleeping. His breathing seemed more erratic. His struggle to take in the air made me want to flee the room at times, but I could not move because I'd committed myself to stay to the end. Instead, I found myself assessing blame, and the what-ifs began to pile up.

I wondered how much my inability to confront the problems early on in our marriage contributed to how things played out? I knew I avoided confronting our problems head-on because we were apart so much of the time. By the time Phillip's patterns of behavior emerged, I was used to weathering the storms in our relationship. I waited things out until they were over so we could get on with life. His capacity to sometimes be so loving endeared him to me, and the cost of confrontation was often more than I could afford emotionally. That, too, played a large part in the dysfunction. I enabled his negative behaviors because I had little understanding of how destructive it was at the time.

Under the Microscope:

49 Awakening Women "An Imbalance of Power Is The Root of All Toxic And Abusive Relationships," Medium, January 18, 2024,
https://medium.com/@leanneoaten/the-imbalance-of-power-is- the-root-of-all-toxic-and-abusive-relationships-ed272faa69ec

CASE FILE 46
Evidence: Post Traumatic Stress Disorder

PTSD, or Post-Traumatic Stress Disorder, is a mental health condition caused by experiencing or witnessing an extremely stressful or terrifying event—in this case enduring financial abuse. Symptoms may include flashbacks, nightmares, severe anxiety and uncontrollable thoughts about the event. This impacts the abused individual far beyond when the abuse has come to an end.[50]

My husband has to sign up for family medical leave, which only pays out a portion of his wages. Our combined incomes aren't nearly enough to pay the bills, so I have to make calls to everyone we have a bill with.

I can't do it. My chest is starting to tighten, and I can feel all the gates and walls and barriers in my head slamming shut. I hate it. I'd rather be attacked by Loki again than make these calls. My whole body is shutting down, and all I can do is clutch the phone while I freeze up.

My skin tingles like it's filled with thousands of needles and my throat starts to close up. It's hard to speak and along the inside of my mouth, words recoil back into my skin.

Sometimes it will take me a week to brace myself enough to pick up the phone and make a five minute, "I'll be late with your money" phone call.

It's a curse.

It triggers panic attacks.

I will do anything to ignore those phone calls.

Avoidance is one of my superpowers. That and making salsa.

With a deep, stabilizing breath I pick up the phone to call our landlord and let them know my husband and I will be late on rent (again).

My fingers won't press the buttons.

A heavy weight bears down on my chest, and I can't breathe. I wish I had a better excuse than 'we're waiting on FMLA to pay us.'

I can't do it. There is an emotion welling up inside me that I don't have a word for. It's a sense of judgment that I can't act like an adult mixed with the shame of my inability to have a financially stable life. I've done something wrong along the way and now I'm acting like a coward as I lay next to Harley and take comfort from him. He doesn't yell at me or tell me what an absolute joke of a human I am. Harley doesn't judge me when I can't do a simple task. All he does is snuggle up next to me like I'm the best human he's ever known and calms my aching heart.

Which I desperately need.

A few years ago my therapist diagnosed me with post-traumatic stress disorder.

Under the Microscope:
50 Yanira L. Rivera Cruz, "Financial PTSD," Center for Financial Social Work, September 1, 2022, https://financialsocialwork.com/essay/financial-ptsd/

CASE FILE 47
Evidence: Chronic Stress

In addition to suffering from PTSD, ongoing, chronic stress can trigger or worsen many serious health problems, including other mental health struggles, heart disease, eating disorders, chronic pain, and other physical struggles such as hair loss and acne.[51]

My life *is* a war.

I'm constantly dodging those topics that will tear me open like a bullet to the chest. I'm always fighting, so my body has to find new and creative ways to get the pain out.

It gives me severe migraines, which in turn trigger seizures. I'm fully conscious when they happen, but I have no control over my body. The seizures didn't start until I got pregnant with my son, but my PTSD has been around since childhood when my father used to pin me against a wall and yell in my face about whatever I'd done wrong. I was so terrified I'd start crying, only to get screamed at for the tears on my face.

I spent years forcing myself not to cry, so I'd freeze like a deer until the yelling stopped. In these moments as I stood silently with my back against the wall, the weight of shame would settle on my shoulders. I was nothing. I was worthless. That knowledge would tighten my chest and prickle all the emotional sensors in my head. I needed to cry, but I didn't dare.

My father never physically struck me, but his words cut deeper than a knife. The ability to freeze correctly and hold my tears in became a narrative that peeled away the layers of my self-worth and set the stage for a life of fear and self-deprecation. When I would discuss this childhood ideology decades later with my brother, he didn't believe me.

Under the Microscope:
51 Bessel van der Kolk M.D., *The Body Keeps the Score: Brain, Mind, and Body in the Healing of Trauma* (Penguin Books; Reprint edition, September 8, 2015)

CASE FILE 48
Evidence: Weaponization of Guilt

Abusers often make their victims feel guilty for their own abuse. They will repeatedly tell the person that the abuse is being done to them because of some failure on the victim's part. They will behave as though the abuse is necessary to correct this failure. In reality, the abuser is making up excuses to justify his actions. The victim is not at all responsible for their behavior towards them.[52]

My husband and I don't want to live here anymore, but we have to work out a payment plan to keep a roof over our kids' heads. I should be able to handle this. Hell, I never should have fallen into this situation in the first place.

If my father could see me now. I'm absolutely certain both disgust and disappointment would be frozen in his ice-blue eyes. He would shake his head because he wouldn't believe his daughter was still making stupid mistakes.

That would lead to the guilt I always felt—that I can't do anything right. Something is obviously wrong with me.

A long time ago, I didn't lose this badly at life all the time. I miss the feeling of a win, of the happiness and sense of accomplishment I once felt, long ago, before my life was railroaded onto a different trajectory.

Under the Microscope:
52 Deborah A. Lee DClinPsy and Sophie James, *The Compassionate-Mind Guide to Recovering from Trauma and PTSD: Using Compassion-Focused Therapy to Overcome Flashbacks, Shame, Guilt, and Fear* (New Harbinger Publications; Illustrated edition, January 2, 2013)

CASE FILE 49
Evidence: Conditional Love

When you have a child, you're supposed to love that child no matter what they do. You're supposed to wholeheartedly support that child while offering correction when needed. But the child should always know that they are loved.

When love is withheld if a child misbehaves, or because a child grows to believe differently than the parent, the result is conditional love. Withholding love this way is abusive.[53]

Despite the elation of becoming a freshman varsity runner, it always felt like I had to prove myself to other people. No matter how many races I won, or how many medals I took home after each meet, in the back of my head I just wasn't good enough. I wanted to get all the way to the state championships, and I wanted to be invited to the Arizona Track & Field meet, a prestigious, invite-only event where high school students from half a dozen southwestern states competed against one another.

When sophomore year started, I still sucked at school. I didn't want to do it, so I did the absolute bare minimum until my grades became Ds. Then my father would stand over me at home and yell until I finished my homework, constantly telling me how horrible a kid I was for not having better grades. He would do this until I was up to a B in my classes, then he would ignore me, and I would slack off again.

As a kid, I really loved my father, but I did everything in my power to escape his notice. I was terrified of him, of getting in trouble, and of the degrading, narcissistic speeches I'd have to endure every time I did something wrong.

So each day I'd arrive at school two hours early to work out in the gym, then stay three hours after school to train on the track.

Under the Microscope:
53 Pam Miller, *Un-Doing Conditional Love: Life Lessons in Love, Loss, & Forgiveness* (Pam Miller Consulting LLC, July 21, 2020)

CASE FILE 50

Evidence: Narcissism

Because a narcissist is the center of their universe, the child of a narcissist is in a bizarre predicament. In the mind of the narcissist, they are simultaneously a projection of themselves and never good enough. This is not something that can be overcome. It is never the victim's fault that the narcissist can't love them properly. The narcissist can only love themselves.[54]

A few days before graduation, my father sat me down at the kitchen table and ordered me to sign a stack of paperwork an inch high. The creamy white paper had so much tiny black text on every page it was almost painful to look at. I never read the documentation, but then I didn't need to. Dad made things very clear from the beginning.

He was ashamed I wanted to attend a state school and not a university. I needed to attend a prestigious university so it would reflect well on him, a man who never even graduated from community college. Don't worry, he had some pretty stellar accomplishments in his life, this just wasn't one of them.

My father had called the college sports committee at my new school to refuse the scholarship and my admission. As if he was the fucking boss of me.

There are no words to describe the utter devastation and rage coursing through my veins that night. I was still seventeen, not yet an adult, and terrified that I'd lose the coolest opportunity I'd ever received, just as I'd lost Arizona.

I fought, maybe for the first time in my life. I desperately wanted to leave home, to keep running, and more importantly, I wanted to get the fuck away from my father.

His anger exploded that night and it turned into a screaming match. I kept my back to the open air so I wouldn't be cornered against a wall, but it didn't matter. Before long,

I was a deer in headlights, too scared of my father's anger to resist. I already carried the weight of wrongness that defined who I was under the family lens, and I was tired of the shame.

So tired.

All the fight went out of me, and I collapsed in tears. He won, and he knew it. He forced the pen into my hand and methodically flipped to each page that needed my signature.

Shell-shocked and on the wrong side of *his* law, I signed the papers, which included large student loans. I now had a federal debt that brought a suffocating weight.

In my later years, I learned of the fight my parents had that night. My mother yelled at him for hours, but in the end Dad won. Just like he always did. After all, he was the head of the house and had control over every big decision. If it wasn't for the family–translation: for *him*–it wasn't happening.

But maybe I could salvage the situation. The next day, I called my intended college several times, telling them I still wanted the scholarship, and that my father had spoken out of turn. It didn't matter. By the time I put in that first call, the college had already given my scholarship to someone else. If I still wanted to attend, I had to take out more student loans to pay for tuition and housing.

The devastation hit me like a speeding train. I'd lost, and there was no way out.

A week later my father accepted a job in Atlanta, Georgia, 1,500 miles away. Before he left, he made sure I understood that part of my enrollment in the university was because I needed to stay here (in Colorado) and take care of my mother and brother. They were perfectly fine, by the way, and didn't need me, but somehow I was responsible for them now, and I had to keep up my grades.

It was a manipulation tactic to keep me under his control. It was now my duty to get a job and help with bills, to attend school in classes with over three hundred students (per classroom), to keep my grades at a B or above, and to keep the family together.

Off to Georgia he went, leaving behind a legacy that would both define and destroy my future.

Under the Microscope:

54 Dr. Karyl McBride Ph.D., *Will the Drama Ever End?: Untangling and Healing from the Harmful Effects of Parental Narcissism* (Atria Books, March 26, 2024)

CASE FILE 51
Evidence: Name Calling

In order to retain their superiority, an abusive person will use language to devalue and dehumanize their victim. This is one of the many types of verbal abuse. Continued verbal abuse can completely damage the victim's self-worth.[55]

My father worked a typical nine to five job. I often didn't start work until four in the afternoon, so our schedules always clashed. I understood his sleep disorder and was beginning to make friends, so every night after work I'd stop at the top of the neighborhood, hang out with Denmark and Douche- Waffle (trust me, this is the nice name for him), then drive home.

Before I hit the last curve to the house, I'd turn off the car and coast silently into the driveway. After taking off my shoes and spending twenty minutes creaking open the car door and nudging it shut, I'd tiptoe to the side of the house, pull out my keys, and spend another ten minutes holding my breath as I silently unlocked the door, inched across the entry, and held the knob twisted all the way tight to close it with a whisper.

I'd moved myself into the basement too, so I never had to travel upstairs to sleep. All the noise would be downstairs, on the other side of the house, and far away from my father. Stepping around every cricket and cockroach, shoes held in one hand, keys in the other, this whole process would finally get me tired enough to fall asleep so I didn't toss and turn on my creaky pull-out couch.

I did this every night for months.

But the shield known as my mother was in California taking care of my grandmother, who was dying from cancer. That's when my father started calling me names.

Whore. Slut.

Thief.

Drug addict.

For reference, I was still a virgin and had never been in the same room as any (non-legal) drug, and the only thing I ever stole was a pocket full of candy at six years old, which my mother still laughs about today.

Every time the slurs slid out of my father's mouth, I tried to defend myself, but a daughter can only take so much.

I packed up the car and moved in with my boyfriend and two best friends. The four of us split the rent, the food, and we never missed a day of work. I might have been poor, but I wasn't completely broke. For the next two years I worked, partied, and tried to forget the life I could have had. My father's words had tainted me, so I began sleeping around, getting high, and I lost every ounce of self-respect I had.

Only work gave me a sense of pride. It was something I could do right, and my boss saw how smart I was. It's why when she got promoted to another store, she took me with her.

Under the Microscope:
55 Lindsay C. Gibson, *Adult Children of Emotionally Immature Parents: How to Heal from Distant, Rejecting, or Self-Involved Parents* (New Harbinger Publications; 1st edition, June 1, 2015)

CASE FILE 52
Evidence: Double Standard

Emotionally abusive people often hold double standards. What is okay for the abuser to do is a terrible infraction when the victim does it. They will then routinely gaslight the victim and play the victim until they cave in and agree with the abuser's double standard. The victim will often question if they were ever right about the double standard to begin with.[56]

I was taken to jail, and the bail was a lot higher than the ticket. The price of everything together turned out to be twenty times higher than the original speeding ticket, and that didn't include impound costs.

That night was the last time I ever saw my car.

My parents arrived the next morning and we had to talk with a thick glass pane between us. I don't remember my mother saying much, but my father yelled at me then said these exact words: "You screwed yourself in, you can screw yourself out."

This from the man who was arrested twice in his teens, and **not** for minor infractions I might add. I won't divulge the nature of his crimes, but his father (my grandfather) bailed him out both times within a matter of hours. I digress.

The moment my father walked out of that room, a bitter resentment lodged itself in my heart, festering with a rage that honestly has never quite evaporated. He has no idea how much that moment still fucks with my head.

Under the Microscope:
56 Lissa Rankin, MD, "The 5 D's of Coercive Control: Double Binds, Double Speak, Double Standards, Double Vision & DARVO," Lissa Rankin, MD, https://lissarankin.com/the-5-ds-of-coercive-control-double-binds-double-speak-double-standards-double-vision-darvo/

CASE FILE 53

Evidence: Spiritual Abuse

Religion can often give hope and support to those who suffer from abuse. But there are also forms of abuse that use spiritual beliefs to control, shame, and humiliate people.  *Unfortunately, for those who do believe, this practice can often interfere with the faith or healthy spiritual growth of the victim.*[57]

I returned to Colorado, and within the first year I got pregnant by my old friend Douche-Waffle. In a religious household, this is the ultimate act of betrayal. My family already criticized me for so many things, including sex before marriage, and with this new revelation, the whore daughter had finally committed the ultimate shameful act.

I'd already had three doctors confirm I was barren and couldn't have children, and I was even on medication for what was believed to be stomach ulcers because I couldn't stop puking stomach bile.

When we finally figured out I was pregnant, I was twenty-seven weeks along. My father ostracized me and sent a very long-winded letter about what a shame to the family I was, a shame to his religious beliefs and all his friends, and that I wasn't fit to be a mother. He ended the letter by telling me to get rid of the child and dump her into the foster system—that she'd be better off.

That man could go fuck himself. Douche-Waffle, too.

News of the pregnancy hit me hard. Getting ostracized from my family devastated me. And when I called Douche-Waffle (the sperm launcher) to let him know I was pregnant, he stopped all communication with me while his family declared me a gold digger. Apparently they're wealthy-something I had no knowledge of.

I'd become the cancer in everyone else's lives, but I knew one truth in my own: no matter how hard I had to work, I would care for my daughter so she would always know how much her mother loved her.

Under the Microscope:
57 "Signs of Spiritual Abuse," W*e*bMD, September 17, 2024, https://www.webmd.com/mental-health/signs-spiritual-abuse

CASE FILE 54

Evidence: Weaponization of Family, Children and Pets

Parental abuse doesn't end when the child is an adult. Instead, the abuse continues, evolving in unexpected ways such as this case, where the abusive father threatens to get custody rights of their grandchild taken away from their child. In any abusive situation, the addition of children makes it that much harder to fully escape the 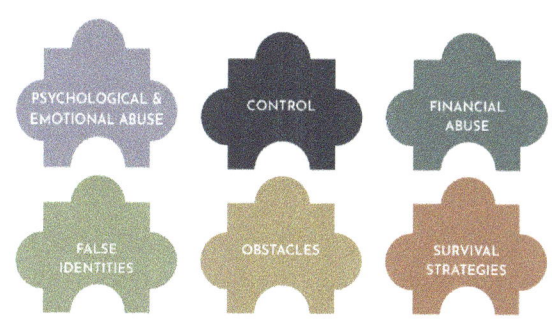 *control of the abusive individual. The fear of risking the child's welfare is too extreme. In some cases, these threats can be avoided. In others, particularly when the abusive person is the other parent of the child, this can get much more frightening.*[58]

We had $0.67 in our bank account and three cans of green beans in the cupboard. I finally debased myself and called my mother to tell her what happened, begging her to let us come home. I would take my father's abuse with a smile on my face if it meant my daughter got to eat.

"You can't," she whispered into the phone. "I love you both with all my heart, but if you come back, your life will be over. Dad will make sure of that."

She didn't even have to explain what she meant—I already knew. My father would destroy me, and he would make sure my daughter was shoved into a foster home where I couldn't touch her.

Something in me died that day. My daughter and I had nothing left. Those haunting words erased the last bits of my self-worth while I clutched the phone in my hand. I'd been a winner once, but all I could hear now was my father's voice. *You're an unfit mother. You need to give your daughter away.*

I almost believed it, until my mother whispered one more thing into the phone. "You'll find a way out. I believe in you."

She hung up the phone.

I just stood there with cold, numbing prickles all over my skin. Dropping the phone, I returned to the small apartment and stared at the curtains for hours. My daughter knew her mother loved her, but it wouldn't be enough. Not for her.

Under the Microscope:
58 Steven Farmer M.A., *Adult Children of Abusive Parents: A Healing Program for Those Who Have Been Physically, Sexually, or Emotionally Abused* (Earth Magic, Inc., January 26, 2016)

GLOSSARY OF TERMS

Abandonment

Abandonment is a form of emotional abuse. Abusers use threats of abandonment as a means of controlling their partners.

Blame Shifting

Abusers deflect blame onto their partners to avoid taking any responsibility for their actions or behavior. This perpetuates a cycle of manipulation, control, and emotional abuse.

Coercive Control

The ultimate goal of abusive behavior is power and control over the actions of another individual. Abusers often display their belief that they should be able to control all elements of the victim's time.

Conditional Love

Abusers use the tactic of conditional love to control the actions and reactions of their victim by promoting the notion that the victim is only worthy of their love if they behave in certain ways. Otherwise the love is withheld and fear is created that victims will risk losing the abuser's affection. Withholding love this way is emotionally abusive.

Controlling Assets

Abusers restrict the use of joint assets to maintain control over their victims. This is a form of financial abuse.

Controlling Employment

Abusers often try to prohibit their partner from working or sabotage their employment or educational opportunities to prevent them from acquiring the financial resources necessary to become independent. This is a type of financial abuse.

Chronic Stress

In addition to suffering from PTSD, ongoing chronic stress can trigger or worsen many serious health problems, including other mental health struggles, heart disease, eating disorders, chronic pain, and other physical struggles, such as hair loss and acne.

Destruction of Self-Esteem

Abusers often take aim at their victim's self-esteem to destroy self-confidence, making their victims easier to control. Victims internalize the negative messages sent by their abusers and begin to believe the false narrative.

Devalued

Abusers use criticisms and rejection to undermine their victim's self-esteem. They blame or insult their victims and put the victims on the defense.

Dominance Hierarchies

Abusers construct a dominance hierarchy based on the status within a relationship they believe is important. The hierarchy is not always consistent which disorients the victim. An abuser's actions indicate whether they believe a person is above or below them in status.

Double Standard

Emotionally abusive people often hold double standards. What is okay for the abuser to do is a terrible infraction when the victim mirrors the action. They will then routinely gaslight the victim and play the victim to reinforce the double standard. The victim will often question if they were ever right about the double standard to begin with.

Emotional Abuse

Abuser's behaviors are motivated by their desire for power and control over their victim. They will use various tactics to manipulate the victim's emotions. Emotional abuse is a broad umbrella of behaviors and tactics used to target a victim's emotions, behaviors, and thought patterns, resulting in hypervigilance, stress, self-doubt, and can lead to chronic mental health issues. The trauma is very real, as the victim is made to feel ashamed, guilty, violated, erased, or silenced into compliance.

Façade of Equality

An abuser will often start off the relationship by presenting themselves as caring, kind and helpful. This makes them appear to be a wonderful partner and creates a sense of trust within the victim. Abusers use flattery and love bombing to convince their victim they are special.

False Self-Identity

Abusers present negative impression of their victims to undermine their self-esteem and create false impressions to bolster their ability to manipulate and control the narrative.

Financial Abuse

Economic abuse includes exerting control over income, spending, bank accounts, shared assets, bills, employment, housing and borrowing.

Financial Gatekeeping

When an abuser makes all the decisions with little to no input from their partner, that is financial gatekeeping. Gatekeeping is the act of trying to control who gets certain resources. In the case of financial gatekeeping, those resources are monetary resources. Sometimes this can involve keeping a partner out of what should be shared decisions about joint finances. This illustrates the abusers need for control and their demonstrative distrust of their victim.

Financial Infidelity

In a relationship, the thoughts, feelings and decisions of both individuals should be taken into account. Not doing so negatively impacts their health and well- being in the dynamics of their relationship and establishes an element of financial infidelity. The abuser's money behaviors cause financial trauma for their victims.

Financial Sabotage

Abusers sabotage their victims' earning potential as a way to prevent them from becoming independent. This is a form of financial abuse.

Financial Trauma

Financial trauma refers to the distress associated with chronic money-related stress cause by the lack of resources. It can be brought on by financial abuse, making it overwhelming to cope with the fears of being homeless or unable to care for yourself, members of your family or pets. This leaves victims in a heightened state of fear, anxiety, anger or depression.

Gaslighting

Abusers use blatant untruths in an accusatory manner to try and deny things they have said, done, or promised. Abusers use gaslighting to deny reality or pretend to have forgotten what actually occurred. The impact makes the victim question their own thoughts and memories and they can become confused, anxious, isolated, and depressed.

Guilt

Abusers instill guilt and shame by preying upon the insecurities caused by slowly eroding the victim's sense of self-esteem. They make demands of their victims and question their loyalty making them doubt their self-worth.

Humiliation

Abusers use humiliation to disorient their victims by degrading them. Verbal assaults such as belittling, ridiculing, or devaluing has a negative impact on the way the victim perceive themselves.

Insults

Abusers often use verbal insults to belittle their victims. This is another method that is employed to chip away at the self-esteem of the victim. Eventually, the victim begins to believe the cruel things being said about them, and it makes it easier for the abuser to continue bringing their victim down.

Intimidation

Abusers use intimidation to instill fear of harm to their victim. The abuser demonstrates they are capable of violence. They can threaten harm to children, animals or the victim. They use intimidation to make victims compliant and force them into submission.

Isolation

Abusers isolate their victims to control their activities and social interactions. By influencing where their victims go and who they communicate with, they reduce a person's access to other people and resources.

Lying

Abusers use lying as a tactic to gain power and control over others. Lying not only confuses the victim and those unaware of the lie, but it establishes an alternate reality that allows them to shirk from their responsibility. Lying is a form of manipulation of a person or situation.

Manipulation

Manipulation is coercive or unethical behavior driven by the goal of exploiting or controlling another person for their own personal gain.

Minimizing

Abusers impact a victim's self-esteem by dismissing, ignoring, or refuting a victim's thoughts, feelings and experiences. A victim's perspective is undervalued, unimportant, thereby impacting their self-confidence. Victims feeling insignificant and their personalities erase when their abuser minimizes a victim's pain and suffering.

Minimizing Feelings

When an abuser minimizes or invalidates your feelings, they are belittling the victim's perspective of events. This can look like dismissing, ignoring, or downplay your thoughts, feelings and experiences. This is done as a way of making the victim feel unimportant and lose confidence. It helps the abuser maintain their control and keeps the victim from speaking up about the abuse.

Minimization and Rationalization

To avoid responsibility, abusers often deny or minimize the consequences of their actions. They deflect the truth and ignore facts to rationalize their thoughts.

Name Calling

In order to retain their superiority, an abusive person will use language to devalue and dehumanize their victim. This is one of the many types of verbal abuse.
Continued verbal abuse can completely damage the victim's self-worth.

Narcissism

Because a narcissist is the center of their universe, the child of a narcissist is in a bizarre predicament. In the mind of the narcissist, they are simultaneously a projection of themselves and never good enough. This is not something that can be overcome. It is never the victim's fault that the narcissist can't love them properly. The narcissist can only love themselves.

Obstacles

In addition to the barriers abusers create for their victims, they also face a multitude of layers when leaving a domestically abusive relationship. Obstacles include concerns for the safety of children, pets and other family members, finding transitional housing, a lack of financial resources, or negative experiences in the past that cause fear of making matters worse when they suffered retribution, humiliation of a failed attempt at escaping.

Post-Traumatic Stress Disorder

Post-Traumatic Stress Disorder is a mental health condition caused by experiencing or witnessing an extremely stressful or terrifying event. Symptoms may include flashbacks, nightmares, severe anxiety and uncontrollable thoughts about the event. This impacts the abused individual far beyond when the abuse has ended. Abusers can cause PTSD because victims often relive the traumatic events they cause. A person suffering from PTSD may suffer from hypervigilance, functional freeze, isolation, irritability, guilt, or have problems sleeping and finding it difficult to focus.

Power Imbalance

At the root of most abusive relationships, there is a perceived imbalance of power. Maybe one partner makes more money than the other. Maybe one person is more intelligent. Maybe one is older. Maybe one is more beloved in the community. When these perceived imbalances are exploited and manipulated to control the person who is considered to be the less powerful one, this creates the abusive portion of the relationship. Power imbalances do not necessarily make a relationship abusive, but the exploitation of an imbalance does.

Racking Up Debt/Ruining Credit

Abusers can also impact a victim's finances far into the future if they rack up credit card debit or ruin their victim's credit. This makes it harder for the victim to leave, especially if they have no access to or knowledge of the financial accounts. This is a form of financial abuse.

Spiritual Abuse

Spiritual abuse targets spiritual beliefs, ideologies, and laws to control, shame, and humiliate victims into out-of-character behaviors, and in some extreme cases can result in death.

Social Stigma

Social stigmas can create artificial barriers to confronting relationship conflicts. They often conflate issues to allow abusers to manipulate circumstances to deflect responsibility.

Subjugation

In situations of coercive control, abusers slowly break down the self-esteem of the victim. They will subjugate them until the victim willingly puts the abuser before them in all situations, caring for them at the detriment of themselves. This tends to be a slow process and one that is often not even realized by the victim until after they are subjugated for a prolonged period of time.

Technology-Assisted Domestic Abuse

Abusers use technology to track their victims and control access to digital assets, friends, and family. This is a form of coercive control.

The Façade of the "Nice Guy"

Inside the façade of a nice guy hides the same insidious selfish abuser who exhibits coercive control over their victims by appearing to be someone they're not. Their partners know their behaviors show the same sense of entitlement as regular narcissism.

The Good Guy Behavior

Abusers can turn on the charm at will. When they are convinced it will benefit them, there are times when they return to the good behavior that attracted the victim in the first place.

Transactional Manipulation

Since abusers cannot give of themselves freely, they always expect to get something in return, making almost every act between them and others transactional. While some transactional relationships are healthy, it become a problem when manipulation is involved and the abuser only thinks in terms of what they will get in return for their cooperation.

Threats

Abusers intentionally instill fear in their victim by making threats. Threats are a form of manipulation and intimidation which impact a victim by employing psychological or emotional distress.

The Two Faces of Narcissists

Narcissists often behave like they're two very different people. Their public face is lovable, kind, and charismatic. Often, they are well-known in their communities and loved. Their private face is controlling, sometimes cruel, with hair-trigger mood changes. This does even more to throw off the victim, further forcing them to distrust their own understanding of reality. The abuser's external behavior is a shield behind which the abuser hides, protecting them from any accusations that may arise.

Victim Blaming

Abusers will refuse to take responsibility for their actions and often blame the person they are abusing for their own behavior. Outside observers of a situation where the victim remains in an abusive household make assumptions about why the victim stays in the relationship. They use phrases like "it takes two," to suggest the victim has done something to provoke the abuser, justifying their abusers' actions.

Victimhood

Abusers often portray themselves as innocent victims of another individual's hurtful assessment of their character. They abdicate any responsibility for their poor behavior.

Weaponization of Guilt

Abusers often make their victims feel guilty for their own abuse. They will repeatedly tell the person that the abuse is being done to them because of some failure on the victim's part. They will use the abuse to "correct" this failure. In reality, the abuser is making up excuses to justify their actions.

Withholding Money

When an abuser withholds money, it creates a feeling of instability and makes the victim economically dependent upon their abuser. By limiting access to money and the things money can buy, the victim's self-esteem is impacted. In addition, it makes it difficult for the victim to leave an abuser and access safety. This is a form of financial abuse.

Weaponization of Family, Children and Pets

Parental abuse doesn't end when the child is an adult. Instead, the abuse continues, evolving in unexpected ways. In any abusive situation, the addition of children makes it that much harder to fully escape the control of the abusive individual. The fear of risking the child's welfare is too extreme. In some cases, these threats can be avoided. In others, particularly when the abusive person is the other parent of the child, this can get much more frightening, especially in the context of our current court system that often does not look at the trauma of abuse as a mitigating factor in granting custody.

ABOUT THE AUTHORS

KASEY ROGERS

Kasey Rogers spent much of her earlier career working in the commercial film industry in New York City by day and writing a musical in-between film projects. After the birth of her twins, she switched gears to pursue another passion, cooking. That passion led her and her late husband to turn a vacation property in Alexandria, Ontario, into a restaurant. For several years she owned and operated The 2Beans Café and Tearoom in Ontario before moving back to the U.S. Since then, she has written the memoir Our Better Selves: From Secrets and Lies to Healing and Forgiveness, along with a work of literary fiction, The Color of Frost. Along with writing, Kasey is an outspoken advocate for women and speaks about the connection between domestic and financial abuse. Learn more about the I Know Why She Stayed Initiative at: www.iknowwhyshestayed.org

Visit Kasey's website: https://kaseyrogers.com

Sign up for her newsletter: https://kaseyrogers.com/#footer

JUSTINE MANZANO

Justine Manzano is the geeky author of geeky YA novels. Her fiction is tough on the outside and sweet on the inside, like a hard candy with a gooey center, delivered with sass and snark. A freelance editor, she also serves as an Editor-in-Residence at WriteHive. A proud Bronxite, born and raised, Justine lives there with her writer/editor husband, Ismael, her amazing son, and a troublemaking puppy named Trooper. When she's not flailing about her favorite characters and actors, Justine struggles to create her own characters with the hopes someone will flail about them one day. Her award winning debut novel, *The Order of the Key*, a Young Adult Urban Fantasy, has been called "Season 5 of Buffy meets the X-Men," and Justine will likely live happily off of that description alone for the rest of her days.

Visit Justine's website: https://justinemanzano.com

Sign up for her newsletter: https://shorturl.at/w9Uxw

K. J. HARROWICK

K. J. Harrowick is a fantasy and science fiction author with a strong passion for twisted stories that blend grimdark worlds and futuristic technology. She is the co-founder of the *I Know Why She Stayed Initiative*, co-founder of Writer In Motion, a repeat panelist for the WriteHive Annual Convention and the Weeknight Writers Convention, and she's also been a contestant on the gameshow Wordcrash!

Her novel *Bloodflower* has captured readers' hearts by casting a grimdark lens on a colony moon inside a starship, and her co-authored memoir *I Know Why She Stayed*, along with initiative, is helping survivors of financial and domestic abuse regain their independence. With an unhealthy obsession for tacos, cheese, and beer, K. J. also works as a freelance web developer and graphic designer on a broad range of client projects. She is currently working on a science fiction thriller, *The Shadows Beneath*, and a science fantasy romance, *The Mountain and the Moon*, both of which she hopes to release before 2042.

Visit K. J.'s website: https://kjharrowick.com

Sign up for her newsletter: https://kjharrowick.com/newsletter/

ACKNOWLEDGEMENTS

Discussions of domestic and financial abuse can often trigger buried emotions for abuse and trauma survivors. Therefore we would like to thank all the victims who came before us, who gave us language and understanding of these tactics and behaviors so that we could connect to the words, find meaning, and learn to heal ourselves and pave the way for others still caught in the Invisible Trap.

A special thanks to Bob Corrigan, who has been unfailingly supportive in our endeavor. We would also like to thank the medical professionals who study these behaviors and help us broaden our understanding of what happened to us and the trauma we live with, even if we never understand *why* we were the targets.

And finally, to all the people who supported us through our trauma and continue to support others caught in the trap through their love, compassion, and organizations who help survivors. We are your biggest fans, and forever grateful for all that you do.

Kasey, Justine, and K. J.

www.ingramcontent.com/pod-product-compliance
Lightning Source LLC
Chambersburg PA
CBHW080550030426
42337CB00024B/4823